The

A to Z

OF AUTHENTIC LEADERSHIP

26 LESSONS ON PERSONAL AND LEADERSHIP AUTHENTICITY

From Existentialism to Elon Musk,

Nietzsche to Narcissism

Dr Tony Fusco

Copyright © TONY FUSCO 2020
This book is sold subject to the condition that it shall not, by way of trade or otherwise, be lent, resold, hired out, or otherwise circulated without the publisher's prior consent in any form of binding or cover other than that in which it is published and without a similar condition including this condition being imposed on the subsequent publisher.
ISBN-13: 9798678013699

3D Leadership
Consultancy
www.3DLeadership.co.uk

Illustrations by Monika Cilmi.
www.monika149.wixsite.com/monikacilmi

This book has not been created to be specific to any individual's or organizations' situation or needs. Every effort has been made to make this book as accurate as possible. This book should serve only as a general guide and not as the ultimate source of subject information. This book contains information that might be dated and is intended only to educate and entertain. The author shall have no liability or responsibility to any person or entity regarding any loss or damage incurred, or alleged to have incurred, directly or indirectly, by the information contained in this book.

T.L.T.

CONTENTS

PREFACE .... *i*
INTRODUCTION 1
A is for Authenticity 10
B is for Bad Faith 20
C is for Character 26
D is for Diplomatic Leadership 31
E is for Existentialism 38
F is for Frankl 42
G is for Gandhi 52
H is for Hitler 58
I is for Imposture 76
J is for Jung 83
K is for Kierkegaard 91
L is for Logistical Leadership 97
M is for Meaning 105
N is for Nietzsche 118
O is for Organisational Development 122
P is for Pathological Leadership 128
Q is for Qualitative & Quantitative Assessment 152
R is for Rogers 159
S is for Strategic Leadership 168
T is for Tactical Leadership 176
U is for Uncertainty 184
V is for Values 194
W is for Why? 206
X is for Xenophile 215
Y is for Yalom 220
Z is for Zeitgeist 225
ABOUT THE AUTHOR 231

Preface

Well dear reader, it's been an interesting time hasn't it? I began this book early in 2019 and am finishing it as we are all emerging from the pandemic lockdown! How has it been for you? As the drama has both increased and deteriorated externally, how has your own drama been internally? Have you been hunkered down in survival mode or have you had the chance to take stock, and ponder - what of the *old normal*? And what of the *new normal*? Maybe both, as for many, in a very Dickensian way, it has possibly been both the best of times and the worst of times. Have you experienced that polarity? Glancing sideways into an abyss of unknowns, while simultaneously wondering deep down somewhere - is this somehow an opportunity? For re-evaluation and rebirth maybe? What *exactly* is the normal that I'm so intent on rushing back to? In itself there lies a huge question for many of us. How to hold that ambiguity of the unknown and sit with that tension of polarities. Especially when every fibre of our being is straining to predict what next - or scenario-plan, in the business speak of the day. It has been an unprecedented and collective existential shock for many of us, that's for sure.

I have a hopeful notion that the contents of this book may help in this dilemma somehow. Which, of course, is somewhat fanciful as it was started a long time before we had any notion of old-normals and new-normals. However, it does say something about the timeless and enduring wisdom of many of the individuals and ideas presented throughout this short A to Z book. And that is all I am doing. Gathering and presenting a varied assortment of thoughts, lessons and examples from a motley crew of psychologists, philosophers and business and political leaders that I believe might have something useful to say about the subject of personal and leadership authenticity. Some show us what it is whilst others show us what it most definitely isn't! The only real original contribution I make is towards the end of the alphabet where I will share with you some of my own research around Authentic Leadership Development, how it can be done and what it can achieve.

A perhaps obvious point, on a brief A to Z journey of the subject at hand, is that all of the contributors have been brutally edited and summarised. They represent mere sketches of the gigantic figures and ideas that they are and often I give just a sliver of one of their ideas that I believe may offer us something accessible and relevant in our exploration of authenticity and authentic leadership. Towering philosophers such as Kierkegaard and Nietzsche for example get just a few pages each. The psychology lurking behind the leadership of Hitler and Trump, however, get a lengthier treatment because of the frightening lessons they offer. Either way, for each chapter I provide cited references and suggested further reading in the hope that they offer signposts that may help lead you towards the veritable wealth of wisdom that lies behind each of the chapters. I hope at least some of them capture your imagination.

Dr Tony Fusco. Malvern. UK. 2020.

Introduction

Much has been written about Authentic Leadership in the last 15 years but, curiously, most of it seems to go over and over much the same idea. The idea that authentic leadership is about ethics, personal values, understanding your purpose and living and leading in accordance with each of these. In a nutshell this does pretty much some it up. However, such simple ideas don't really say much about the complexities that lie behind them. For example, do you know what your values actually are and crucially do you how and why they were formed? Do you understand and own them or are they unquestioningly adopted from a wider culture or community? Are values the same as ethics or morals? Do you believe your ethics are based on your thoughts, actions or outcomes? Also, if authenticity is summarised as *knowing yourself* and *being true to yourself* do you actually know who or what this self is? Do you have a core self or multiple selves? Should you be true to a stable core self-concept or to your myriad of malleable working self-concepts?

And what of our leadership role models? We all say that Mandela, Gandhi etc were authentic leaders, but why? What was it about them as people and leaders that take us so assuredly to that conclusion? What of Hitler or Stalin, were they authentic leaders? If not, why not? What about Henry Ford, Elon Musk or Donald Trump? Depending on how deeply you wish to consider it, Authentic Leadership can become a deceptively complex idea to untangle. An idea and concept that traverses the fields of psychology, philosophy, sociology and leadership temperament. So, our journey from A to Z will do exactly the same. In 26 bite-size chapters, we will look at a range of ideas and individuals that contribute something of significance to a deeper understanding of what authenticity and authentic leadership actually are. Herein, you will not find a definitive model of authentic leadership, but rather a journey around the idea that helps our understanding of it. A journey guided by the ideas of philosophers, the theories of psychologists and the examples of leaders themselves. We will consider a usual example of authentic leadership in Mohandas Gandhi, but we'll also look at the natural but very different leadership temperaments of such leaders as Elon Musk, Henry Ford, Kofi Anan and Red Adair. Plus, we'll consider the pathological leadership of Messrs Hitler and Trump! Aside from some of my own research around authentic leadership development, it is not my purpose to introduce more thought or theory around authentic leadership. My intention is to capture some of the highly relevant ideas of others that already exist, to hopefully provide an entertaining and illuminating way of understanding authentic leadership. Here is a brief summary of what's to come.

Chapter 1: A for Authenticity – a definition of what authenticity is and a (slightly dystopian) view of the challenges to personal authenticity that may lay ahead in our modern online world.

Chapter 2: B for Bad Faith – Jean-Paul Sartre's idea of Bad Faith and how modern life leads us easily away from living an authentic life to the surrender of our own self-authorship.

Chapter 3: C for Character – a psychological theory suggesting how our own personal temperaments inform our leadership intelligence.

Chapter 4: D for Diplomatic Leadership – first leadership intelligence case study, from the interpersonally orientated mind and leadership of the UN's Kofi Annan.

Chapter 5: E for Existentialism – our first foray into a philosophy of how we contemplate the idea of existence itself. Ostensibly heavy stuff, but in reality, all too human – and indispensable in our enquiry into authenticity and authentic leadership.

Chapter 6: F for Frankl – brings existentialism to vivid life through the first-hand experience of a psychiatrist who answered back to life his view of *its* meaning, while living the nightmare of the Nazi concentration camps.

Chapter 7: G for Gandhi – one very small side of the Mahatma's character that inspires – his insistence on and continual pursuit of truth.

Chapter 8: H for Hitler – *the* inevitable question when it comes to authentic leadership. So, we take a tour of the psychopathologies that informed his leadership and hopefully answer emphatically the question why (I think) he was NOT an authentic leader.

Chapter 9: I for Imposter – the imposter syndrome we all suffer to varying degrees in various way. Where does it come from and why, paradoxically, does it mainly afflict high achievers?

Chapter 10: J for Jung – what does the man right up there with Freud have to offer the concept of authentic leadership? Perhaps the idea of the *shadow*. That within us that we want to disown or deny and project outwards onto others. It can complicate anyone's relations but arguably none more so than leaders in positions of high influence.

Chapter 11: K for Kierkegaard – what is your truth and where does it come from? Is it appropriation or approximation? From without or within? If you don't have a truth you would die for, do you at least have a truth to live for?

Chapter 12: L for Logistical Leadership – our second leadership intelligence case study where we consider the conservative and duty-bound leadership of Henry Ford.

Chapter 13: M for Meaning – which Viktor Frankl suggests is at the authentic heart of *everything!*

Chapter 14: N for Nietzsche – difficult to know where to start. So, we'll start (and end) with his proclamation that *'God is dead'* - so what is man to do?! If there is nothing higher underwriting the meaning of your life you are thrown back onto yourself to decide that for yourself. What are you to do?

Chapter 15: O for Organisational Development – Back down to earth with a bump! What is the place of leadership development in modern-day organisations?

Chapter 16: P for Pathological Leadership – looking inside the mind of the psychopath and exploring the possibility that the leader of the free world actually is one?!

Chapter 17: Q for Quantitative v Qualitative – analysis of why and how we measure leadership development and authentic leadership development specifically.

Chapter 18: R for Rogers – self-reflections on personal authenticity from a master humanistic psychologist.

Chapter 19: S for Strategic Leadership – lesson three on leadership intelligence from the inventive and far-reaching mind of Elon Musk.

Chapter 20: T for Tactical Leadership – a final lesson on leadership intelligence from the bold and adventurous Red Adair.

Chapter 21: U for Uncertainty – a leader's ability to deal with conflict, contradiction and complexity ultimately comes down to their personal maturity.

JFK shows how, through his sensitive management of the Cuban missile crisis.

Chapter 22: V for Values – arguably what forms and informs any leadership. But exactly what are they and where do they come from? *Spoiler* – they come from your own personal autobiography. And the better you know them in your past, the better you can own them in your present.

Chapter 23: W for Why? – why engage in authentic leadership development anyway? What exactly are the benefits? Some research findings.

Chapter 24: X for Xenophile – how authentic leadership development brings leaders into more close and meaningful contact with those they lead. More research findings.

Chapter 25: Y for Yalom – insight into the conditions that create successful authentic leadership development group-coaching from a master existential psychologist.

Chapter 26: Z for Zeitgeist – how the collective existential shock of a world pandemic can lead us to a more meaningful and authentic engagement with life.

It was my dissatisfaction with the academic and professional 'treatment' of authentic leadership that led to the idea of this book. To me it seemed redundant to attempt to conceptualise authentic leadership without due consideration to what great thinkers have said on the matter for eons. I understand business scholars want to capture the 'essence' of authentic leadership and boil it down into a neat set of traits, behaviours or competency frameworks! It's what they do and have done with the models and theories of; Transformational Leadership, Transactional Leadership, Situational Leadership, Servant Leadership, Contingent Leadership, Ethical Leadership etc. And still we wonder what is the secret behind great leadership? It's even been tried with Authentic Leadership, though I'm somewhat heartened to report, with some backlash. By definition, authenticity does not sit on or within any framework of anything. It emerges from an individual not a construct. We often think about the easy archetypes of Nelson Mandela or Martin Luther King. But what about Churchill or Franklin Roosevelt? What of Steve Jobs or Bill Gates? I would argue that all are their own indomitable variation of an authentic leader … without having ever come in contact with a leadership competency model! The point in sum is that ... *what makes leaders great, at any level, are their differences and not their similarities.*

Authenticity

A is for **Authenticity**

"There is a certain way of being human that is my way." [1]

Authenticity has been explored and debated since antiquity and yet somehow seems more relevant today than ever. The onslaught of implicit and explicit messages showing us who we could or should be leaves increasingly little room for us to ponder who we *actually* are. It takes no small amount of effort to quieten the cacophony of modern life just long enough to hear your own voice within it. The maelstrom of social media and News24 also makes it tantalisingly easy to let your mind be made up for you as to who you are and what you believe. In his book *In Search of Authenticity* [2] Jacob Golomb describes

---

[1] Taylor, C. (1996). *The Malaise of Modernity*. Anansi Press. Ontario.

[2] Golomb, J. (2012). *In Search of Authenticity: Existentialism from Kierkegaard to Camus*. Routledge. London.

authenticity as "*...a protest against the blind, mechanical acceptance of an externally imposed code of values*" (p.11) saying we have to "*...create our authenticity... it is not delivered to us by higher authorities*" (p.25). He suggests authenticity is about matching up to and living in accord with self-chosen internal standards. In this way authentic people create individual values, purpose and direction for their lives that can't be understood purely in terms of external acceptance or comparison. Nor can they be objectively right or wrong if they accurately represent who you are, they can only ever be subjectively measured and judged by your own internal standards. And try as it might, the shiny online world cannot, in reality, replace that judgement... yet!

But by the same token, being authentic, means we have to take full responsibility for these values and standards and the related choices and decisions they involve. And for this reason alone, it is perhaps understandable why some people struggle with the uncertainty and angst this can create preferring to shelter within the norms of an existing cultural, social or religious system that offers them the warmth and security of a *human huddle*. However, if as an individual you can tolerate the slight chill of uncertainty, you are rewarded with a self-authorship that means you are in control of yourself and your life and are able to give to both a coherent sense of meaning and purpose. And so, authenticity is not judged so much by *what* you do, but more *how* and *why* you choose to do what you do. In, *The Malaise of Modernity* [3] Philosopher Charles Taylor succinctly summaries this definition of authenticity,

"There is a certain way of being human that is my way. I am called upon to live my life in this way, and not in imitation of anyone else's. This gives a new importance to being true to myself. If I am not, I miss the point of my life, I miss what being human is for me" (p.28-29).

In this book, Taylor emphasises the point that when we create the unique design of our lives, we have to do so while in constant battle with the pressures of a postmodern world that tries to shape and conform us to its own design. Similarly, in *The Saturated Self* [4] Prof Kenneth Gergen forewarns of the problems of modernity that challenge man's search for authenticity. Gergen introduced several prophetic

---

[3] Taylor, C. (1996). *The Malaise of Modernity*. Anansi Press. Ontario.

[4] Gergen, K. J. (1991). *The Saturated Self: Dilemmas of Identity in Contemporary Life*. Basic Books. New York.

terms that relate to the idea of authenticity in the modern world. For example, he coined the phrase *technologies of social saturation* which he uses to describe the forces that immerse us ever deeper into the socially connected world and expose us to endless images and opinions of others. He warns that this increased *populating of the self* could lead us to experience a *vertigo of unlimited multiplicity* that in time could even lead to the *erasure of the individual self*,

"Emerging technologies saturate us with the voices of humankind. As we absorb their varied rhymes and reasons, they become part of us and we of them. Social saturation furnishes us with a multiplicity of incoherent and unrelated languages of the self. This fragmentation of self-conceptions corresponds to a multiplicity of incoherent and disconnected relationships. These relationships pull us in myriad directions… the very concept of an authentic self… recedes from view as the fully saturated self becomes no self at all" (p.6-7).

It is sobering to consider Gergen wrote this when the worst offenders were probably SKY-TV and MTV, quite some time before the full force of the wired-world was unleashed. So, what of the post-social-media world? Will it really impact our sense of self in the way these 20th-century philosophers predict? Neuroscientist Susan Greenfield certainly thinks so and in *The Neuroscience of Identity* [5] she proclaims,

"If as a species our most basic and valuable talent is a highly sensitive adaptability to our environment, then screen-based life with prolonged surfing, virtual reality gaming and social-networking cannot fail to have a transformational effect on our mental states and the eventual consciousness of the human species" (p.92).

Susan Greenfield is Professor of Synaptic Pharmacology at Oxford University and Director of *The Institute for the Future of the Mind*. As one of Britain's leading neuroscientists, Prof Greenfield focuses her research on how the brain gives rise to a sense of human consciousness and in particular what our world of rapid technological change means for the human brain and human nature. She proposes that a stable and consistent sense of identity comes from an overarching organisation of what she calls *unique temporal sequencing*. Within this, she believes, nests a hierarchy of extensive and dynamic neural circuitry that responds to

---

[5] Greenfield, S. (2011). *You and Me: The Neuroscience of Identity*. Notting Hill Editions. UK.

every moment of action, reaction and interaction with the outside world. But she asks,

"What if that outside world were to change in an unprecedented way? How will the brain, evolved as it is to adapt to whatever environment confronts it, be modified by the unprecedented impact of biotechnology, nanotechnology and info-technology. Will identity remain a robust and continuous experience, or change in some new way, or – bleakest of all – cease to have any real meaning altogether?" [6] (p.111).

Then in *ID: The Quest for Meaning in the 21st Century* [7] Greenfield asks what she believes to be the most important question humanity can now ask itself: how might new technologies impact our brains in completely novel ways that actually transform us as people? What will happen to our minds – our unique identities? She believes nothing short of the fact that *"...our identity as twenty-first-century individuals is in crisis..."* (p.117) and that in postmodern life the inner

---

[6] Greenfield, S. (2011). *You and Me: The Neuroscience of Identity.* Notting Hill Editions. UK.

[7] Greenfield, S. (2008). ID: *The Quest for Meaning in the 21st Century.* Hodder & Stoughton. London.

sanctum of the individual self is under threat like never before. The dangers, she believes, lie in the eventual erosion of *the firewall* between our inner and outer life. This increasingly frayed edge where our Facebook and Instagram accounts finish and the outside world begins.

As our brains, our minds, and our sense of self, are all inextricably interlinked with an ongoing dialogue with the outside world, Greenfield suggests it might become increasingly difficult to protect our true self from our online exaggerated ideal self and ponders what will happen when the air-brushed *cyber us* starts to elbow-out the *real us*:

"Until now, the adult mind was the product of a dialogue between environment and self, and this dialogue allowed for pauses, self-reflection and the slow but sure development of a robust internal narrative… which amounts to what we call identity. In contrast, an unremitting [screen-based] environment… will present the polar opposite: a scenario that displaces a robust inner sense of identity in favour of one that is externally constructed and driven… therefore less robust and more volatile" (p.133).

What will happen when we spend most of our time living in a passive state simply observing and reacting to a constant flow of incoming and fleeting screen sensations? To be constantly stimulated by the present moment, absorbed by only the here-and-now life of the screen. This must surely have an eventual impact on our unique, temporal sense of identity; one that evolves and develops over a timeline through our past, present and future. Living this unique narrative over a lifetime, with these three interconnected domains is key to our developing sense of self. So, what happens when we give up this evolving life of cause and effect for one of little or no consequence trapped perpetually in the present? What then happens to the neural connectivity of our brains, our neuronal landscape that has been shaped and strengthened through a lifetime of interaction with the world. What happens to the shaping of our brain that reflects our unique life lived when that life becomes mostly lived only in the present and through a screen? Could it even obliterate our narrative of personal identity?

"The burgeoning technologies of the twenty-first century have the potential for bending the brain in new ways and opening it up to manipulation as never before in the history of Homo Sapiens. The biggest question is whether the result of such unprecedented brain changing might be reflected ultimately in an unprecedented transformation in human identity" (p.35).

Ultimately, Greenfield believes that the increasingly interlinked and pervasive technologies of info-technology, nanotechnology and biotechnology could have the potential to dismantle this firewall and the traditional means of individual demarcation and thus *obliterate the individual* altogether. It was disconcerting to hear Gergen talk in the late 20th century about the sense of self *fraying around the edges* and claiming that *"...it is the achievement of authenticity that the technologies of social saturation serve to prevent"* [8] (p.203). If identity is to become an increasingly transparent, fragile and questionable entity as the century unfolds, then it is even more foreboding to hear Greenfield talk, not of the self-receding or fraying, but of its inevitable obliteration, potentially by mid-century. She emphasises, *"... identity gives meaning to our lives... it is one of the most important concepts for humanity to appreciate,*

---

[8] Gergen, K. J. (1991). *The Saturated Self: Dilemmas of Identity in Contemporary Life.* Basic Books. New York.

preserve and understand' [9] (p.139). We have been warned…

Further Reading:

Aboujaoude, E. (2012). *Virtually You: The Dangerous Powers of the E-Personality*. Norton & Co. London.

Carr, N. (2010). *The Shallows: How the Internet is Changing the Way We Think, Read and Remember*. Atlantic Books. London.

Greenfield, S. (2014). *Mind Change: How Digital Technologies are Leaving their Mark on our Brains*. Penguin. Random House. UK.

Greenfield, S. (2005). *Tomorrow's People: How 21st Century Technology is Changing the Way We Think and Feel*. Allen Lane. Penguin Books. UK.

---

[9] Golomb, J. (2012). *In Search of Authenticity: Existentialism from Kierkegaard to Camus*. Routledge. London.

Bad Faith

B is for **Bad Faith**

> *"The one who practices bad faith is hiding a displeasing truth or presenting as truth a displeasing untruth. What changes everything is the fact that in bad faith it is from myself that I am hiding the truth."* [10]

In his best-selling book *Everything is F*cked* [11] Mark Manson recounts, in his typically modern irreverent style, the myth of Pandora's box. Pandora came down to earth with a box the gods had given her along with explicit instructions that it not be opened. But sure enough, man opened it and from it sprang all of the world's ills; death, disease, hatred, envy and according to Mark Manson – Twitter!

---

[10] Sartre, J. P. (2001). *Jean-Paul Sartre: Basic Writings*. Routledge. London.

[11] Manson, M. (2019). *Everything is F*ucked*. Harper Collins. New York.

We saw in the opening chapter how the pervasive use of social media and other forms of virtual life may begin to have a profound impact on our personal identity by around mid-century. But ahead of that we are already witnessing some of its deleterious effects on our authentic sense of self by sometimes surrendering to it in a way Jean-Paul Sartre would describe as *Bad Faith*. Bad faith is the term Sartre uses to describe how we live when we fail to take full responsibility for ourselves, our lives and our choices. We sometimes choose to hand over that responsibility to others to determine what or who we should be. Previously this may have entailed handing over such authority to fixed value systems or social roles such as family, job, religion or history and let these decide for us who and what we are. Sartre says that the reality of our freedom is simply too burdensome for us to bear, hence his famous quote about man being *condemned to freedom*. He thinks we simply find it too anxiety-provoking or effortful to confront our freedom and accept the responsibility for realising our own identity, so we refuse to freely make ourselves what we are. When we fully realise the extent of this responsibility to author ourselves, it creates within us a deep sense of anxiety, even dread. And so, rather than live life as an authentic self-defining project we run from this discomfort and live our life in some form of bad faith.

Sartre says that although we know we are free and have the capacity to make our own choices we mask this capacity from ourselves by conforming to the fixed image others have of us or, more often the case these days, by constructing an image we want others to have of us. There have always been various routes into bad faith available to us, but modernity now comes with the optional extra of an entire virtual existence. In this digital existence there are many ways for denying our freedom and responsibility for self-authorship and endless opportunities for succumbing easily into a life of bad faith. So, now Sartre's idea of bad faith is taking an interesting turn. Instead of hiding from the pressure and discomfort of having to self-author our existence by adopting fixed mechanistic roles understood and accepted by society, we nowadays achieve the same bad faith by creating fluid, ephemeral identities tentatively offered to the wider world to see what we get back in terms of recognition, admiration and acceptance. Sartre believed that in bad faith we adopt roles which mask our freedom. Perhaps now we also adopt multiple roles or identities to mask the freedom and responsibility we have to create our real authentic identity.

As Sartre says, facing our freedom requires facing our responsibility but as we can't bear to face this responsibility, we deny our freedom. And how easy it is these days to deny ourselves this freedom by paradoxically engaging in a perverse kind of freedom that enables us to be anyone we want and create a number of immediate forms of digi-selves that we think the world will approve of and accept. This in turn lifts our sense of dread by easing the burden on us to choose and commit to who and what we authentically are. We are ultimately responsible for our way of being in the world despite the multiple ways in which we can pretend, mimic or play at being who we could be. Authenticity then, according to Sartre, is to turn away from the temptation and comparable ease of bad faith and recognise, accept and embrace this personal freedom and responsibility.

This is of course easier said than done, especially in organisational life. As social-political places organisations simply drip with opportunities for acting in bad faith. Sometimes it almost feels like a prerequisite for the job or that our careers depend on it. The case may be even harder for leaders who have to be many things to many different constituent groups and stakeholders. We will see throughout the alphabet of this book examples of leaders who both succumb to and resist bad faith. First though, let's try and bring this very abstract philosophy of Jean-Paul Sartre back down to something a little more tangible and accessible, i.e. personality. It can be argued that if you are living and leading in a manner congruent with your own genuine personality and values then you are living and leading authentically and in good faith. Personality can be thought of as a mix of what nature has endowed us with and what nurture has then added to. Our nature is based on the raw ingredients that we are born with and in personality terms is called our temperament. Even long before life experience has got to work on their very young children most parents will recognise that their offspring have been blessed, or perhaps cursed, with a particular temperament or character. By the time these toddlers become our political leaders or captains of industry this temperament will begin to show itself in very clear terms. Conveniently for us, terms that can be neatly categorised into just four different types of character and temperament. We meet four leaders throughout this book who demonstrate to us in very vivid terms how these different types of leadership temperament can manifest, but first, beginning in the next chapter, we will look more closely at the idea of temperament and its allied leadership intelligences.

Authenticity and authentic leadership are not binary. They're not either-or, they're more or less. To be fair, we live in a world that tempts us incessantly into bad faith. But what are your own 'ouch' moments? The moments you think - shit! My response to that could or should have been very different. What are the moments when you think that was a four-out-of-ten when it really should have been a six/seven-out-of-ten? When you walk away from such situations how well do you think you represented the real you? Assuming you could return to that situation again, what would you do differently, as the real you? As authenticity is not binary – on a scale of 1 to 10, if it wasn't a 10 (and when is it?) what could you do next time to dial it up from 2 to 4 or from 6 to 8? These reflections and actions can help lead us away from bad faith and towards increased authenticity.

Further Reading:

Sartre, J. P. (1973). *Existentialism & Humanism*. Methuen. London

Sartre, J. P. (1989). *Being and Nothingness*. Routledge. London

C is for **Character**

The temperament a leader is born with is probably a more fundamental determinant of their behaviour than their entire constellation of extrinsic influences.

The idea that humans are born with fundamentally different temperaments has been with us for over 2000 years. It is assumed they are rooted in our biological heritage and emerge irrespective of race, gender, intelligence or nationality. It was the Greek philosopher Plato who first observed the four main characters of man which he introduced as the iconic, pistic, noetic and dianoetic temperaments. The iconic temperament was endowed with an artistic sense and the pistic with common sense. The noetic temperament was characterised by an intuitive sensibility and the dianoetic by a reasoning sensibility.

He suggested each of these temperaments played a particular role in society. The iconic, with their artistic sense played the art-making role in society. The pistic with their common sense played the care-taking role. The noetic with their intuitive sensibility played the moral role and the dianoetic with their reasoning sensibility played the logical role. Plato's student Aristotle then added to this and suggested that these four temperaments seek their happiness either through sensual pleasure, acquiring assets, through exercising moral virtue or through logical investigation. Later still, the Roman physician Galen observed four seemingly identical temperaments calling them the sanguine, the melancholic, the choleric and the phlegmatic characters; four temperaments that he described as optimistic, doleful, passionate and calm. Through the 18th century various philosophers similarly identified these four main temperaments, the likes of Adickes, Spranger, Kretchemer and later psychologists such as Jung and Fromm and later Myers and Kiersey. Although each looked at the four temperaments from slightly different angles, time and again, the four broad same personalities emerge from their observations. The final iterations, and the ones we relate to here, are proposed by Keirsey and are called Artisans,

Guardians, Idealists and Rationals. Respectively they house four different leadership intelligences; *tactical, logistical, diplomatic* and *strategic*. The book *Presidential Temperaments*[1] offers examples of each from US history. The venturesome Tactical leader for example would be Teddy Roosevelt or JFK. The steadfast Logistical leader is epitomised by George Washington. And the far-sighted Strategic leader includes the like of Thomas Jefferson and Abraham Lincoln. Interestingly however, there has never been a Diplomatic leader of the US, with the possible recent exception of Barack Obama.

Social factors such as family background, education, economic and social status naturally play a significant part in character development. As do the circumstances of any one particular time in history one is born into. However, the temperament a leader is born with is probably a more fundamental determinant of their behaviour than this entire constellation of extrinsic influences. As such, similarities in temperament can cut across differences in personal history, social background and current context, in the same way that differences in temperament can clearly separate people of very similar backgrounds. For example, leaders from any background sharing the Strategic intelligence would automatically resonate as if on the same wavelength *"The farm boy Eisenhower would have no difficulty making sense of the aristocrat Jefferson's' absorption in designing both the buildings and the curriculum of the University of Virginia"*. As would be the case of those sharing the Tactical leader intelligence, for example, *"The charismatic aristocrat Kennedy may have disliked the hard-living rural Johnson, but each could readily take the other's measure, and knew what to expect from the other"* [12] (P.12).

So, your *leadership* temperament is an extension of your *personal* temperament. It is your natural predisposition towards certain patterns of behaviour that will appear consistently throughout your life. Your temperament comes from your biological inheritance as your character results from the interplay between your biology and your environment. Although social context inevitably makes a strong impression on your character, this character and its associated pattern of behaviour will arise from and be consistent with this predetermined temperament. Insight into how such temperaments influence a leaders' behaviour, will be offered throughout the alphabet by four-character

---

[12] Choiniere, R., & Keirsey, D. (1992). *Presidential Temperament: The Unfolding of Character in the Forty Presidents of the United States*. Prometheus Nemesis Book Co: US.

studies representing each of the four Temperaments and their allied leadership intelligence. Under 'L' we will consider the captain of industry, Henry Ford as an example of the sober, society-serving Logistical leader. Under 'S' we look at the visionary leadership of Elon Musk as our example of the Strategic leader. And under 'T' we observe Red Adair as the bold and adventurous Tactical leader. But first, in the following chapter 'D', we will look at the exemplary work of the UN's Kofi Anan to illustrate the interpersonal intelligence of the Diplomatic leader.

If after reading these brief leader profiles, you are curious to know your own leadership temperament you can complete Keirsey's Temperament Sorter in his excellent book *Please Understand Me II* [13].

Further Reading:

Barr, L., & Barr, N. (1989). *The Leadership Equation*. Eakin Press. USA.

Pearman, R. R. (1998). *Hardwired Leadership*. Davies-Black. USA.

---

[13] Keirsey, D. (1998). *Please Understand Me II*. Prometheus Nemisis Book Co. US.

DIPLOMATIC LEADERSHIP

D is for Diplomatic Leadership

"As the first secretary general elected from the ranks of the organisation, I came into office with a hard-won appreciation for the limits of our powers, but equally determined that we would not give up in the face of setbacks – that we could do better and would do so in the name of the peoples for whom the Charter of the United Nations was written." [14] Kofi Anan.

Diplomacy is the ability to deal with people in a skilled, tactful and interpersonally sensitive manner. The Diplomatic leader uses their verbal skill and fluency to mediate interpersonal conflicts. With an instinct for seeking the common ground, an ability to interpret each side's communication in a positive way and a gift for putting themselves in another's place, the Diplomatic leader is well-equipped for the difficult task of influencing people's actions and attitudes. As leaders they inspire people to grow, they smoothly settle

---

[14] Annan. K. (2012). *Interventions: A Life in War and Peace.* Penguin. UK.

differences and are ever looking to forge unity among the people around them. Such individuals may be given to diplomatic leadership as they are deeply disturbed by division and discrimination. Conflicts and disputes unsettle them, and they prefer to focus on a shared experience and common truths. Perhaps for this reason the most famous idealist Diplomatic leaders are those who forged changes in equal rights and social justice, using themselves as the main instrument of their leadership, such as Nelson Mandela, Mohandas Gandhi and Martin Luther King. In this chapter however, we will see what this form of leadership looks like by studying diplomatic leadership as demonstrated by Kofi Anna, Ghanaian diplomat and United Nations 7th Secretary General.

From his first day in office, Kofi Annan reminded the heads of state that the first words of the UN Charter did not refer to them but, 'We the Peoples' and stated that he wanted to bring the UN closer to the people they were there to serve. Instead of leading an organisation dedicated to the governments of the world, Annan wanted to put the world's individuals squarely at the centre of everything they did. He wanted a UN fit for the 21st century that could respond to the needs of the individual and stand for the principle that even national sovereignty could not be used as a shield for genocide or gross violations of individual human rights. His idealistic and diplomatic leadership intelligence firmly set his leadership agenda.

Annan came to power seeking to catalyse action across a wide range of issues – HIV/AIDS, women's education, African development, post-tsunami relief work, advancing human rights and the rule of law. Determined that sovereignty be both a matter of right and responsibility, he was to dedicate his efforts towards achieving a United Nations that would step-up rather than stand-by and rise to the demands of a new century and be guided by a purpose greater than just the self-protection and self-interest of states. This reflected his conviction that while humanitarian intervention was a moral and strategic imperative, even 'allied' military intervention without legitimacy or foresight could potentially be as destructive in its consequence, as the evil it purports to confront.

Immediately upon taking office Annan found himself drawn into a vortex of conflicts that threatened entire societies with destruction. After an early visit to post-war Rwanda in 1998, Annan began a process of reform in UN peacekeeping. His approach was to first acknowledge a recent history of failure, fully and honestly, accepting that the atrocities of the civil war there was a stain on the organisation. But they were also, he believed, a lesson that they could use and turn into a powerful and productive instigator of reform. And it did, changing the doctrine, strategy and decision making in peacekeeping. For example, going forward he gave the UN peacekeepers on the ground who witnessed violence against civilians, authority to intervene within their means, while accepting their limitations to decisively change the course of a civil war. He knew this responsibility remained that of the member states and the UN Security Council.

While Diplomatic leaders are exquisitely attuned to the human side of their leadership, this also means an uncompromising focus on the individuals perpetrating harm through their leadership, even extending to individual heads of state. Through the trials of peacekeeping in Somalia, Rwanda and Bosnia, Annan had arrived at the conclusion that human rights to life and security were being increasingly threatened by conflicts internal to states themselves and not just across borders. He believed that this meant the UN had to reframe the relations between citizens and government. It needed to convince the broader global community that sovereignty had to be understood as contingent and conditional on states taking responsibility for the security of their own people's human rights. With his vision of putting individual rights back at the heart of the UN's charter, Annan wanted to make clear to the global community that the rights of sovereign states to non-interference in their internal affairs could not override their populations right to freedom from systematic abuses of their human rights. He believed there should be a deterrent created by the UN that included the threat of a military response to such violations. If states knew that frontiers were not an absolute defence and that the UN Security Council would take action to halt crimes against humanity, they may not embark on such atrocities expecting sovereign impunity. He warned in a speech to the General Assembly in 1999 *"If the collective conscience of humanity cannot find in the UN its greatest tribune, there is a grave danger that it will look elsewhere for peace and for justice"* [15].

It can be common to mistake the diplomatic leaders' empathy and compassion for softness or weakness. However, where rights and moral values are transgressed, they can show a tough and uncompromising streak. Even as the world's most senior diplomat, Anan believed that the UN should not be just a pacifist organisation and that there were

---

[15] Annan. K. (2012). *Interventions: A Life in War and Peace.* Penguin. UK.

times when force was both necessary and legitimate in the pursuit of peace. Annan would urge often for the intensification of diplomacy, but also for this to be backed by a credible threat of force where necessary.

Testimony to his personal presence, integrity and skill in communicating and trust-building, Annan became a central node of diplomatic communications worldwide. During his time as UN leader, from the Middle East to East Timor, it seemed he was the only one that all the different parties in the various conflicts all felt comfortable speaking with, in trust and confidence. Politically and tactically this gave him a better and more up-to-date understanding of the state of play and position of each party, with many sharing their interests, knowledge and even intelligence with him. All of this in turn enabled him to broker agreements with more insight and impact than almost anyone else involved, and he took advantage of this. One of his favourite diplomacy tricks was his 'leader-roundtable' meetings. Annan was well aware that to be a head of government is to be trapped in the paraphernalia and pressures of office and to be in the midst of countless aides and advisors. Many times, he had seen this interfere with and undermine agreements based around otherwise rational collective interest. But he also knew that when he got these leaders on their own, he would invariably find that even the most intransigent of them would prove a lot more reasonable and responsive. So, he brought this particular form of diplomacy into various UN summits. He began to set up round table discussions with various leaders to examine crucial issues but set the requirement that only the heads of states and governments would be in attendance, with no aides or advisors accompanying them. He wanted these key individuals stripped of their domestic political distractions that the civil servants, political advisors and presidential handlers bring with them to negotiations. Tellingly, the staff hated these meetings, but the leaders loved them. Such is the skill and tact of the Diplomatic leader.

How about you? Are you in your element in the interpersonal realm? Working out the different connections and motivations between the individuals and groups within your own constellation of influence? If your 'leadership home' is a fundamentally person-centric one it will influence all around you – for better and for worse. If this is you, then be the intuitive sage-leader you are… just ensure you have a team around you who are also focussed on the less personnel orientated, but nonetheless vital performance and task related work!

E is for **Existentialism**

"Existentialism not only talks about, but calls people to, the authentic attitude." [16]

Existentialism is the philosophy of existence, not of things that exist, but of existence itself. If you've ever asked yourself "what does life mean?" or "why am I here?" then you've dabbled in Existential Philosophy! And you're in good company.

In Ancient Greece students of this philosophy included the almost mythical figures of Socrates, Plato and Aristotle. It was after these greats however, that Existentialism really came of age when in the 19th-century belief in God was on the decline and emphasis on Science was beginning to dominate. The

---

[16] Cooper, D. E. (1990). *Existentialism*. Blackwell. Oxford. UK.

Industrial Revolution was overturning traditional forms of social order and the world was becoming a more industrialist, scientific and secular place. During this time, particularly in continental Europe, philosophers were beginning to ponder earnestly, the human condition. In particular the issues of human existence such as individual freedom, responsibility and quite literally, the meaning of life. Nesting amongst these issues lay the question of personal authenticity and the question of how to live an authentic life. Most Existentialists agree on the importance of living authentically, embracing personal freedom and responsibility and living in accordance with who one really is. Although they knew it to be a struggle, they believed it a worthy one. Living authentically was uncomfortable. Far easier, in Sartre's bad faith, to let one's life conform to all the pre-existing meanings and values that the world, readily, offers. The crowd can, after all, be a comfortable and comforting place, requiring considerable strength if one is to avoid its absorption. But ultimately, if you live only by the opinions or expectations of others, you are failing to be authentically you.

For Existentialists, authenticity means living in a way that reflects accurately your own internal template of who you are. You understand that template and make choices that design a life consistent with it. So, living an authentic life means setting yourself free of the constraints of a world that tries to form that template for you and dictate how your life should be lived. It is about taking full responsibility for the choices and decisions that will forge your own individual path through life. Summarised beautifully by the existential psychotherapist Irvin Yalom who we meet under 'Y',

"The existential world view... embraces rationality, eschews supernatural beliefs, and posits that life in general, and our human life in particular, are thrown alone into existence without a predestined life structure and destiny; that each of us must decide how to live as fully, happily, ethically, and meaningfully as possible" [17] (p.202).

This is a profound view! But one that fundamentally informs our perspective as we move forward. Authenticity, and in turn authentic leadership, depends quite literally on how we decide to live (and lead) as - *fully, ethically, and meaningfully as possible*.

There are numerous existential thinkers and writers

---

[17] Yalom, I. D. (2008). *Staring at the Sun: Overcoming the Terror of Death*. San Francisco: Jossey-Bass.

who have asked what this actually means, including; Soren Kierkegaard, Friedreich Nietzsche and Irvin Yalom, and each of these we meet throughout the alphabet. But first we meet an individual who asked and answered such profound existential questions in the nihilism of the Nazi concentration camps, the Swiss Psychiatrist – Viktor Frankl.

Further Reading:

Blackham, H. J. (1952). *Six Existential Thinkers*. Routledge & Keegan Paul Ltd. London.

Fusco, T. et al (2015). *An Existential Approach to Authentic Leadership Development: A Review of the Existential Coaching Literature and its relationship to Authentic Leadership*. The Coaching Psychologist. 11, 2. 61-71. The British Psychological Society.

Kaufman, W. (1975). *Existentialism: From Dostoevsky to Sartre*. A Plume Book. Penguin. US.

Nauman, St. E. (1972). *The New Dictionary of Existentialism*. The Citadel Press. New Jersey.

Solomon, R. (1974). *Existentialism*. The Modern Library. Random House. New York.

F is for **Frankl**

"Everything can be taken from a man but one thing: the last of the human freedoms – to choose one's attitude in any given set of circumstances, to choose one's own way." [18] Viktor Frankl

An essential figure in any discussion of personal meaning and authenticity is the psychiatrist Viktor Frankl. The reason is twofold. First, his entire school of thought is based around *Mans Search for Meaning* [19], which is a fundamental issue in existential authenticity. Second, he developed his thinking as a camp prisoner and survivor in WWII. This couches his views in an

---

[18] Frankl, V. E. (1985). *Man's Search for Meaning*. Simon and Schuster. London.

[19] Frankl, V. E. (1985). *Man's Search for Meaning*. Simon and Schuster. London.

experience that should help give us all perspective and certainly makes him an individual worth listening to. His view however is somewhat different to the normal meaning-seeking perspectives. He believes that you don't *ask* of life what it's meaning is for you, he firmly states that you should *answer* to life what meaning you will give *it*. In exploring his philosophy further, I think it useful to hear in some of Frankl's own words how he developed and applied his beliefs in the extremes of the Nazi death camps. He begins by telling us how his own sorry journey literally began,

"The carriages were so full that only the top parts of the windows were free to let in the grey of dawn. The engine whistle had an uncanny sound, like a cry for help sent out in commiseration for the unhappy load which it was destined to lead to perdition. Then the train shunted, obviously nearing a main station. Suddenly a cry broke out from the ranks of the anxious passengers 'there's a sign… *Auschwitz!*'" (p.27).

After his arrival at Auschwitz, Frankl observed different psychological stages that would unfold in the prisoners. In the first stage the newly arrived prisoners experienced painfully torturous emotions;

the longing for home and loved ones and the disgust at everything else they witnessed around them. The second stage however, once entrenched in camp life, was one of apathy in which the individual experienced a kind of emotional deadening that desensitised them to all the death and pain that surrounded them. This self-defence mechanism dimmed reality and allowed all a person's efforts to focus on the central task of survival. This regression to a primitive form of mental life seemed essential in hanging on to what Frankl called their *provisional existence*:

"A man who could not see the end to his 'provisional existence' was not able to aim at an ultimate goal in life. He ceased living for the future. Therefore, the whole structure of his inner life changed, signs of decay set in" (p.51).

Frankl himself combatted this by trying to recreate in his mind the manuscript of his life's work that had been confiscated when he arrived at the disinfectant chamber in Auschwitz. He recalls how this intensification and focus on an inner world helped many prisoners find a refuge from the desolate emptiness of camp life. Remembering once working in a freezing trench many miles from camp, Frankl recalls,

"The dawn was grey around us; grey was the sky above; grey the snow in the pale light of dawn; grey the rags in which my fellow prisoners were clad and grey their faces. I was struggling to find the reason for my sufferings, my slow dying. In a last violent protest against the hopelessness of imminent death, I sensed my spirit piercing through the enveloping gloom. I felt it transcend that hopeless, meaningless world, and from somewhere I heard a victorious 'Yes' in answer to my question of an ultimate purpose" (p.60).

Frankl came to understand that trying to survive in a world that no longer recognised the value of human life, making them just objects to be worked then exterminated, easily robbed a man of his will and his values. But if he didn't struggle against this in a last effort to salvage some self-respect, he would lose the feeling of being an individual with personal value and inner freedom. He saw that being treated as a nonentity eroded these values as the average prisoner became increasingly degraded to nothing. But was this decline inevitable and unavoidable, he questioned. He wondered about human liberty and spiritual freedom and whether man could internally escape his grim external reality. He observed,

"The experiences of camp life show that man does have a choice of action. There were enough examples, often of a heroic nature, which proved that apathy could be overcome. Man can preserve a vestige of spiritual freedom, of independence of mind, even in such terrible conditions of psychic and physical stress" (p.86).

Frankl gives examples of men who would comfort others or give away their last piece of bread, and witnessing this led him to the conclusion summarised in his most famous quote that *"Everything can be taken from a man but one thing: the last of the human freedoms – to choose one's attitude in any given set of circumstances, to choose one's own way"* (p.86). He believed that there were always choices to be made, every hour of every day, that offered the opportunity to make decisions that would determine whether or not a man would renounce his dignity and inner freedom. He concluded that, despite the external conditions, the sort of person the prisoner became was not just the result of camp influences alone, but also as a result of their inner decision, *"Fundamentally, therefore, any man can, even under such circumstances, decide what shall become of him – mentally and spiritually*" (p.87). Witnessing kind behaviours in camp clearly demonstrated to Frankl that this last inner freedom can be salvaged. But he also observed that those who let go of it also lost their hold on life and eventually fell victim to the camp's degenerating influences. He said, you knew when a person had lost this will to live because you would see them smoking their own cigarettes, usually kept to trade for bread or watery soup, just so they could enjoy something of their last days.

Through his experience in, not one but, four concentration camps, Frankl developed his psychology and philosophy of life's meaning. He came to realise that you don't ask of life what it's meaning is for you, but rather life asks you, and "*Woe to him who saw no more sense in his life, no aim, no purpose, and therefore no point in carrying on. He was soon lost*" (p.98). Frankl came to realise that what was needed was a fundamental change in the attitude towards life. When life asks such a question of us, Frankl believes we can only answer for ourselves and not for life generally, as each man's destiny is unique,

"We had to learn ourselves... that it did not really matter

what we expected from life, but rather what life expected from us. We needed to stop asking about the meaning of life, and instead think of ourselves as those who were being questioned by life" (p.98).

Fundamentally, Frankl believes that the search for the meaning of human existence is the primary motivational force in man and that in the concentration camps you knew those who believed there was a meaningful task waiting for them to fulfil, as these were those most likely to survive. Of his own experience he says,

"When I was taken to the concentration camp of Auschwitz, a manuscript of mine ready for publication was confiscated. Certainly, my deep desire to write this manuscript anew helped me survive the rigors of the camps I was in. For instance, when I was in a camp in Bavaria, I fell ill with typhus fever, I jotted down on little scraps of paper many notes intended to enable me to rewrite the manuscript, should I live to the day of liberation" (p.127).

Frankl also believes that mental health is based on a certain degree of tension between what someone has achieved and what they still have to achieve, who someone is and who they are still to become. He believes that this tension is more important to mental well-being than the idea of an equilibrium or tensionless state. He says that what man actually needs is the struggling and striving for a freely chosen and worthwhile goal. What he needs is not homeostasis, but the calling of a latent meaning waiting to be discovered and fulfilled. Man's main concern is not just to achieve pleasure or avoid pain, but to seek meaning. Frankl also believes that this is not a general and abstract meaning, but a very specific and concrete one, unique to each individual and their own particular life and circumstance. It may change but it will never cease to be.

Frankl proposed a thought experiment *"Live as if you were living already for the second time, and as if you had acted as wrongly the first time as you are about to act now!"* (p.132). An experiment, he says, that allows us to imagine that the present is past, and the past can yet be changed and amended. This is allied to another of Frankl's key ideas. He says that the potentialities in our own lives only remain as such until the moment they are realised and actualised. At this moment they are transformed into realities and as such can be delivered safely into our past *"For in the past, nothing is irretrievably lost but everything is irrevocably stored*" (p.143). We are therefore constantly making choices about the mass of potentialities that face us. Which will we assign to non-being and which will we actualise and deliver safely into our past? Frankl asks, which of our choices will we turn into *immortal footprints in the sands of time*? In this way his philosophy of the passage-of-time is a very positive one, believing that *having been* is the surest form of being – the possibilities in our futures no more precious than the realities in our past, of choices made and meanings fulfilled.

Therefore, facing the mass of potentialities that confront you, you have just one excruciatingly simple but difficult decisions to make. Which of all of these, do you want to assign to non-being? And which of these do you want to deliver safely into your past? Your own *immortal footprints in the sands of time*? And you should choose wisely for these potentialities will be never be irretrievably lost but *irrevocably stored* safely into your own personal history.

Further Reading:

Fabry, J. B. (2013). *The Pursuit of Meaning: Viktor Frankl, Logotherapy and Life.* Purpose Research. US.

Frankl, V. E. (1978). *The Unheard Cry for Meaning: Psychotherapy and Humanism*. Hodder Stoughton. UK.

Frankl, V. E. (2000). *Man's Search for Ultimate Meaning*. Basic Books. New York.

Frankl, V. E. (2014). *The Will to Meaning: Foundations and Applications of Logotherapy*. Penguin. USA.

Gould, W. B. (1993). *Frankl: Life with Meaning*. Brooks Cole. USA.

G is for **Gandhi**

"Gandhi's presence in the twentieth century, a century that perfected the art of extermination, is weirdly arresting. His life seems peculiarly unhoused in the violent landscape of his times. How, by what twist of historical fate, did this frail, ungainly man… evoking a faded, archetypal memory of saintliness, wander into the modern world?" [20]

So opens the Introduction to Gandhi's autobiography, and if there was ever an embodiment of an authentic leader then it would have to be Mohandas Gandhi. His entire adult life was given to personal service and public justice, prompting George Orwell to comment that *his whole life was a sort of*

---

[20] Gandhi, M. K. (1982). *The Story of My Experiments with Truth.* Penguin Books: London.

pilgrimage in which every act was significant. Many words come to mind when we think of Gandhi such as humility, service, sacrifice and non-violence, but for me the one that stands out, and the one I believe to be most relevant to authenticity, is *truth*. We know of course that Gandhi was a highly principled man but among all of the principles he held and lived, truth for him was what he called the *sovereign* principle. "… *truth is not only truthfulness in word, but truthfulness in thought also, and not only the relative truth… but the absolute truth. I am prepared to sacrifice the things dearest to me in pursuit of this quest*" (p.15). A quest Gandhi called the *summon bonum* of life – the highest good.

In the 1880s Gandhi trained as a barrister in London and in the 1890s began practising law in South Africa. Here his very first public speech was on the subject of observing truthfulness in business. This was a tough message to promote to that profession in that place at that time. He recalls,

"I had always heard the merchants say that truth was not possible in business. I did not think so then, nor do I now. Even today there are merchant friends who contend that truth is inconsistent with business. Business, they say, is a very practical affair, and truth is a matter of religion; and they argue that practical affairs are one thing, while religion is quite another. Pure truth, they hold, is out of the question in business, one can speak it only so far as is suitable. I strongly contested the position in my speech and awakened the merchants to a sense of their duty" (p.126).

As a law student Gandhi had heard that his chosen profession was known as a liar's profession, but he was adamant that he was not going to gain money or position through lying. This principle was sorely tested in South Africa. There he knew that many of his legal opponents would tutor their clients. Gandhi always resisted this saying he only ever wanted to win cases if his client was in the right. He would warn potential new clients that he would not take on their case if it were a false one. As a result, he built such a reputation that clients only brought their 'clean' cases to him and took their 'doubtful' ones elsewhere. On one occasion when he was conducting a case before a judge in Johannesburg, Gandhi discovered that his client had been lying to him when he took the witness stand. Without hesitation he asked the magistrate to dismiss the case, much to the astonishment of both the judge and the opposing counsel. Needless to say, his reputation soared, as did his Law business.

It was also in South Africa that Gandhi began to formulate his philosophy of civil disobedience.

Initially, the English term passive-resistance was used for this, but he found this too narrow and therefore unsatisfactory. Eventually he settled on the term *Satyagraha* meaning Sat = truth and Agraha = force. His resoluteness in the face of the social injustice he saw in South Africa and his unwavering commitment to resistance through non-co-operation, led one friend to write to him saying *"I should not be surprised if one of these days you have to go to the gallows for the sake of truth"* (p.321). He never reached the gallows, but he did suffer much violence against him along with time in prison for his unfaltering adherence to *Satyagraha* and his insistence on truth-force.

Gandhi believed that his life experience had taught him that there was no other God than truth. Both his outer and inner lives were devoted to a pilgrimage in both a search for and an insistence upon it. This, he said, gave him ineffable mental peace, *"I had long since taught myself to follow the inner voice. I delighted in submitting to it. To act against it would be difficult and painful to me"* (p.134). He also believed that morality should be the basis of all things and that truth was the substance of all morality, *"The deeper the search in the mine of truth, the richer the discovery of the gems buried there"* (p.206). He concludes his autobiography, *The Story of My Experiments with Truth,* [21] by saying that if he has not convinced the reader of *the indescribable lustre of Truth* then it is the vehicle at fault, not the great principle itself.

In the 1960s the renowned psychoanalyst Erik Erickson travelled to India to research a psychological biography he was to write called *Gandhi's Truth* [22]. On one occasion he asked the gathered congregation how they had each met Gandhi. He then asked them how they would describe the essence of his presence? Erikson reported that the most universal answer to the question about what one felt around Gandhi was *"in his presence one could not tell a lie"* (p.63).

A key feature of authentic leadership is how it makes followers feel. They are not diminished, they grow. They are challenged to be their best self. They absorb the example set before them. Gandhi's refusal to compromise on the truth clearly impacted all those around him.

Do you know how people talk about being in your presence? What do you think they say about you

---

[21] Gandhi, M. K. (1982). *The Story of My Experiments with Truth.* Penguin Books: London.

[22] Erickson, E. H. (1969). *Gandhi's Truth.* Norton & Co: New York.

when they're not in your presence? What do you think people say they'd feel uncomfortable doing or saying in your company? Do you think they know what you stand for… and will not stand for? Does it matter to you if they do or not? Do you think it matters to them whether they do or not?

Further Reading:

Gandhi, M. K., & Desai, V. G. T. S Ganesan. (1928). *Satyagraha in South Africa*. Madras.

Herman, A. Bantam. (2008). *Gandhi & Churchill: The Epic Rivalry that Destroyed an Empire and Forged Our Age*. London.

H is for **Hitler**

"It was his ability to convince others that he was what he was not, that saved him from insanity." [23]

In our exploration of authentic leadership, we must now move from an embodied saint to the devil incarnate, as whenever there is discussion about the authenticity of famous historical leaders the name Adolf Hitler inevitably arises. By way of a chapter spoiler, I will say that in my opinion (and that of others) Hitler wasn't an authentic leader. He was a deeply divided individual who battled with a pathology and duality that dominated his personality, his ideology and his leadership and undermined any

---

[23] Langer, W. C. (1972). *The Mind of Adolf Hitler: The Secret Wartime Report.* Basic Books: NY.

possible integration of an authentic self.

Hitler had a very complex and contradictory psyche. He was a man torn between feelings of omnipotence and vulnerability, creativity and destructiveness, pragmatism and fanaticism, industry and lethargy, bravery and cowardice, unimaginable cruelty and bizarrely even some kindness [24]. While he appeared as a messiah to the German people, he was also in many ways infantile and vulnerable, beset by childish fears and neurotic compulsions. Outliving five siblings was probably a key factor in the formation of his belief that he was destined for greatness and chosen by Providence to fulfil some grand, important mission. It is also reasonably hypothesised that the brutal childhood he experienced at the hands of his father contributed to the shame, guilt, mistrust and hatred that would in turn lead to a Borderline Personality Disorder that would go on to wreak a colossal revenge on a despised world [25, 26, 27, 28, 29].

---

[24] Waite, R. G. L. (1977). *Adolf Hitler: The Psychopathic God*. Basic Books: New York.

[25] Bromberg, N. (1971). *Hitler's Character and its Development: Further Observations*. American Imago, 28, 289-303.

[26] Bromberg, N. (1974). *Hitler's Childhood*. International Review of Psychoanalysis, 1.

[27] Langer, W. C. (1972). *The Mind of Adolf Hitler: The Secret Wartime Report*. Basic Books: NY.

Attempts at formally diagnosing psychological pathology, conducted remotely without direct access to the individual concerned, is of course considered tentative and speculative. However, there have been two notable attempts at this endeavour conducted during and shortly after World War II. The first was conducted in 1943 by the American Psychoanalyst Walter Langer who prepared a report on Hitler for the U.S. Office of Strategic Services[30]. The second remote diagnosis was conducted by the prison psychiatrist at Nuremberg Dr Douglas Kelley [31] who undertook extensive interviews with 22 members of Hitler's immediate Nazi circle. Both men concluded that Hitler could be classified, in the terms of the day, as Paranoid Psychoneurotic.

In addition to these psychological assessments there was also a recorded physical diagnosis in Hitler's medical records. These are reports collected by the

---

[28] Kernberg, O. (1967). *Borderline Personality Organisation*. Journal of the American Psychoanalysis Association, 15, 641-685.

[29] Kernberg, O. (1970). *Factors in the Psychoanalytic Treatment of Narcissistic Personalities*. Journal of the American Psychoanalysis Association, 18, 51-85.

[30] Langer, W. C. (1972). *The Mind of Adolf Hitler: The Secret Wartime Report*. Basic Books: NY.

[31] Kelly, D. (1947). *22 Cells in Nuremberg: A Psychiatrist Examines the Nazi Criminals*. New York.

U.S. Military Intelligence, now in the U.S. National Archives, which include the results of four ECG's taken between 1940 and 1944 showing quite clearly that Hitler suffered from 'rapidly progressive coronary arteriosclerosis'. This medical evidence could explain his physical deterioration later in life for which other explanations including Parkinson's and Syphilis remained unsubstantiated. Importantly this condition can also produce personality changes where even psychologically stable individuals can become delusional and paranoid. The general consensus by those qualified, (including Langer, Kelley and Bromberg) was that Hitler displayed tendencies consistent with, what is now termed 'Borderline Personality Disorder'.

Individuals with such a Borderline Personality can often function with great effectiveness even though they are considered mentally ill. Their pathology is different from neurosis and less severe than psychosis and lays somewhere on the border between the two, hence the term. These individuals characteristically show narcissistic, paranoid tendencies and are very suspicious and distrustful of other people. They consider themselves especially privileged individuals and fantasise about their own omnipotence and believe they have the right to exploit people for their own gain. Along with their sense of omnipotence though, they also harbour deep-seated self-doubt and insecurity. Borderline individuals can also show infantile and child-like oral aggression and demandingness, a well-known characteristic of Hitler's. They have a narcissistic inflated opinion of themselves and harbour a considerable need for admiration from others.

Overall though, they have a confused sense of identity that they are unable to fully integrate, having what the renowned psychologist Erik Erikson termed 'identity diffusion'. This diffusion and splitting of the self can result in the dramatically opposing personality traits mentioned earlier. For example, they can be at once; cruel and kind, creative and destructive, sensitive and tough. This is described by Kernberg as having two distinct selves, equally strong but completely separate. Importantly, Borderline personalities don't want to reconcile these two selves either, as they seem to be not just a defect of the ego, but a defence of it as well. It is said that the main purpose of this duality is to protect a weak ego from the anxiety of choosing between its two violent extremes and so it accepts them both. This splitting, of course, doesn't solve the problem but weakens the ego further by reinforcing this identity diffusion.

Hitler suffered considerably from this confused and contradictory sense of identity and one way of compensating for the tormenting self-deception was always having to appear in control. He often talked of his iron-will, his coolness under pressure and it was clear that his whole political system was basically a vehicle to extend this control over others.

Finally, Borderline Personalities reinforce this splitting through something called introjection and projection. They introject good into themselves and they project bad onto others. Hitler introjected all the aspects of Aryan good into himself and all bad onto others, especially the Jews. This splitting can create a terrifying split world view, as it did with Hitler, of irreconcilable forces of good and evil at war. Hitler externalised this internal conflict and felt compelled to fight the encircling enemy that he believed constantly threatened him. Whilst this brought untold misery for others, it served as a crucial defence mechanism for himself, preventing ultimate mental disintegration and collapse. This Borderline Personality defence explains why Hitler never actually crossed over into full-blown psychosis. While his fantasies may have been like that of many other mentally disturbed people, there was one crucial difference - instead of being given psychological treatment, he was given political power.

He was able to externalise his inner conflict - rationalise it, project it and then even proclaim it as official national policy. His internal neurosis and psychic needs were transformed into an external reality that would institutionalise his own hatred and create a government dedicated totally to warfare and the complete extermination of the Jews.

Despite introjecting all the good he saw in the Aryan, Hitler remained plagued by self-doubts about his own physical strength and masculinity. His appearance did not really fit his image of the brutal, all-conquering Aryan he preached of so often. He was effeminate in many ways, was of ambiguous sexuality and along with sadistic had clear masochistic tendencies as well. As a result, every defeat unnerved him so much he would have to pursue further battles and victories as proof that he was in fact the ice-cold and ruthless leader of his fantasies. He was obstinate and brutal, and prided himself on what he considered these masculine traits. However, psychiatrists who study these traits suggest their roots lay not in mastery but in anxiety and as a defence against one's own feelings and fears of inadequacy.

Historians agree that Hitler's stubbornness sometimes served him well tactically in the short term. But ultimately as a long-term strategy, it only helped bring disaster and defeat. This need for overt masculinity meant he always had to take the offensive. He could never consider a defensive strategy or tactical retreat for any reason whatsoever. If there was one word, other than Jew, that was certain to send Hitler into one of his famous rages it was *capitulate*. Even when a victory had been won, this would not stop him from attacking further. He is quoted as saying,

'Wherever our success ends, it will always be only the point of departure for a new struggle, we shall attack, and it is immaterial whether we go 10 km or 1,000 km beyond the present lines. For whatever we gain, it will always be only a starting point for new battles' [32] (p.61).

War wasn't forced on a reluctant Hitler, the war existed *within* him. His Borderline Personality gave him the severe aggressive stirrings and paranoia that made him feel the need to destroy potential enemies before they destroyed him. His private fears of inadequacy and weakness meant war could give him the opportunity he so desperately needed to prove his

---

[32] Hitler, A. (1961). *Hitler's Secret Book* (T. Taylor, Intro.; S. Attanasio, Trans.). London: Grove.

strength. However, these fears could never be allayed, and so war became the sole purpose of the Reich. In the end, it was less painful for him to see this Reich and his Motherland destroyed than it was for him to personally capitulate. Eventually, when he could not secure his victories over the Russians or the Western Allies, he began his ultimate campaign to secure his victory over the Jews with his death camps. This was the only front left in which he could assure himself victorious. Dr Langer recognised this weakness in Hitler, and long before knowledge of the death camps emerged, had anticipated Hitler would compensate for his defeats with increasingly ruthless acts of brutality and destruction. He predicted,

'Whatever else happens, we may be reasonably sure that as Germany suffers successive defeats Hitler will become more and more neurotic. Each defeat will shake his confidence still further and limit his opportunities for proving his own greatness to himself. In consequence he will feel more and more vulnerable and will probably try to compensate for his vulnerability by continually stressing his brutality and ruthlessness' [33] (p.278).

---

[33] Langer, W. C. (1972). *The Mind of Adolf Hitler: The Secret Wartime Report*. Basic Books: NY.

Given such credibly informed reports and interpretations, we can reasonably conclude that it was Hitler's Borderline personality and associated pathologies that more informed his leadership rather than a strong, genuine, enduring and authentic sense of self. He never actually possessed the personal qualities of strength and integrity that he projected. He believed in his mission to deliver a new supreme nation, but the reasons for it and the methodologies chosen to achieve it were not of sound mind, but of a fractured mind that continued to deteriorate to the end. It was predicted, should he have lived to witness the total collapse of his vision, unable to keep together his disparate and warring personality, he would have probably collapsed into full-blown psychosis.

We end with a quote, once again from Langer (1972), that coherently summarises the difference between an authentic-self and a pathological-self and gives what I believe to be the qualified answer to the question – was Hitler an Authentic Leader?

"Hitler likes to believe that this (Fuehrer) is his true self, and he has made every effort to convince the German people that it is his only self. But it is an artefact. The whole 'Fuehrer' personality is a grossly exaggerated and distorted conception of masculinity as Hitler conceives it. The 'Fuehrer' personality shows all the earmarks of a reaction formation that has been created unconsciously as a compensation and a cover-up for deep-lying tendencies that he despises. This mechanism is frequently found in psychopaths and always serves the purpose of repudiating the true self by creating an image that is diametrically opposite and then identifying oneself with the image. It is his ability to convince others that he is what he is not that saved him from insanity" [34] (p.201).

Narcissistic Leadership

Of all of Hitler's many abnormalities, perhaps his most 'normal' abnormality was his narcissism. Although Hitler talked of a thousand-year Reich, he didn't even appoint a successor to take it on even one more generation. What happened to his motherland after him did not ultimately concern him too much, as he himself wouldn't be part of it. Therefore, it was easy for him to proclaim his razed earth policy when he knew his own campaign was doomed. For all the work done resurrecting Germany, it was all done in honour of the Fuehrer. What actually happened after him, was of little concern to him.

---

[34] Langer, W. C. (1972). *The Mind of Adolf Hitler: The Secret Wartime Report*. Basic Books: NY.

Psychologists and psychoanalysts believe a certain amount of narcissism is healthy, even necessary, for an infant's natural healthy growth. It gives them the self-confidence and self-assurance to wean themselves from their mother and start to individuate themselves and grow their own separate identity.

However, if this process is for some reason interrupted and their development is arrested at this natural narcissistic stage, it prevents them from naturally separating, differentiating and distinguishing themselves. If the child experiences any additional trauma during this period, then their emerging self-concept can be damaged leading to an 'injured self'. This can perhaps occur through the child being rejected by a cold and uncaring mother which leaves them emotionally hungry with an exaggerated need for admiration and love in later life [35]. Interestingly, however, even the seemingly contrary experience of an overprotecting and adoring mother can create similar problems. This is because a compulsive and intrusive narcissistic mother can still represent a form of rejection in that they don't allow the infant to individuate and

---

[35] Post, J. M. (2004). *Leaders and their followers in a Dangerous World: The Psychology of Political Behaviour.* Cornell University Press: Ithaca.

naturally separate from them. It is all about them and so their child must remain part of them.

The legacy from this particular type of arrested development is a narcissistic personality. This personality formation is typically characterised by an immense sense of self-importance, grandiosity and omnipotence. This personality is preoccupied with fantasies of extreme success, power and brilliance. But along with these preoccupations, this personality also develops a huge sense of entitlement and expectation of special and favourable treatment. All of this requires constant feeding through attention and admiration and leads to something called the 'mirror-hungry' personality,

"Mirror-hungry leaders require a continuing flow of admiration from their audiences to nourish their famished selves. Central to their ability to elicit admiration is an ability to convey a sense of grandeur, omnipotence and strength" [36] (p.191).

And so, the narcissist leader needs to nourish that

---

[36] Post, J. M. (2004). *Leaders and their followers in a Dangerous World: The Psychology of Political Behaviour.* Cornell University Press: Ithaca.

famished self in displays designed to get the attention of others. However, no matter how much and how positive the response, they will never be satisfied and so will continually seek new audiences to get the attention and recognition they crave, think of the Hitler and Trump political rallies. As I write, Trump has announced his first rally after three months of lockdown. Even weeks before any other indoor gatherings will be allowed, he is content to pack 20,000 of his fan-base into an indoor arena, with all of the health implications that entails, just so he can bask in their adoration and nourish his injured and famished self.

Narcissism exists on a scale that ranges from a normal narcissistic *personality style* to an abnormal narcissistic *personality disorder* [37]. The relatively normal narcissistic *personality style* is not uncommon in occupations such as law, medicine, sports and entertainment. Leaders with a narcissistic *personality disorder* at the other end of the scale, are more often to be found, perhaps unsurprisingly, in business and politics.

Such leaders themselves have developed a *fearful-dismissive* attachment style. This means they have

---

[37] Sperry, L. (2003). *Handbook of Diagnosis and Treatment of DSM-IV-TR Personality Disorders.* (2nd Ed). Brunner- Routledge: New York.

difficulty in cooperation or reciprocal social interaction and appear self-indulgent, demanding and aggressive in their interactions. Their leadership style might at first appear self-confident and nonchalant, but these individuals are extremely vulnerable to criticism, or even just being ignored, and are likely to respond with rage to the slightest criticism or lack of loyalty that might shake their fragile self-confidence, *"Noncontingent love and presumptive control of others is expected and even demanded. Totally devoid of empathy, these individuals tend to treat others with contempt and rage if entitlement fails"* [38] (p.158).

Such demandingness, on the one hand and lack of empathy on the other, means narcissistic leaders only really have superficial relationships with shallow emotional ties. They will use others to meet their own needs but remain wary and dismissive of them or jealous and paranoid. Jealousy and paranoia of course being a fundamental characteristic in the leadership of Hitler, Stalin, Saddam Hussein, Gaddafi and Assad. Such luminaries would be what is called *Malignant Narcissists* which are individuals who engage in aggressive actions to nourish their self-esteem needs -

---

[38] Sperry, L. (2003). *Handbook of Diagnosis and Treatment of DSM-IV-TR Personality Disorders.* (2nd Ed). Brunner- Routledge: New York.

typical of most despots, tyrants and dictators.

By comparison the likes of Trump probably have a mere *Exaggerated Narcissistic Personality Disorder* similar to that of former US President Nixon, who in *Richard Nixon: A Psychobiography,* Vamik Volkan describes for us:

"With Richard Nixon we see exaggerated narcissism, but not malignant narcissism. Nixon organised his personality at such a level that he had an exaggerated need to be 'number one' in his own eyes as well as in the eyes of others, to maintain his self-esteem, and to avoid the anxiety of acknowledging his hungry self" [39] (p.91).

As and when this defensive façade failed him, he is said to have regularly felt and reacted; *humiliated, enraged, envious and paranoid.*

As I conclude this book, we are witnessing Trump's leadership during the US race riots following George Floyd's death. The nation and its people are crying out for a leader to acknowledge their plight, offer empathy and understanding, to soothe, to unify and to begin to heal the nation. The absence of any hint

---

[39] Volkan, V. D., Itzkowitz, N., & Dod. A. W. (1997). *Richard Nixon: A Psychobiography.* Columbia University Press: New York.

of this coming from The White House is influencing how events are unfolding and may ultimately determine their final destination. And the sole reason for this radio silence from The White House is because the individual in the Oval Office is simply incapable of any of the above – as we'll hear later in the alphabet it simply gives him 'brain freeze'! But all of this is illustrative of perhaps the most worrying aspect of the Narcissistic Personality Disorder that pertains to leadership, *"The illusion of specialness, disdain for others' views, and a sense of entitlement lead to an underdeveloped sense of social interest and responsibility"* [40] (p.159).

Narcissistic leadership is antithetical to authentic leadership, because it is driven by, not just any personality disorder, but a personality disorder that is characterised by **an underdeveloped sense of social interest and responsibility**. With these leaders, however charismatic their leadership style or cause may first appear, look and listen very closely and you will see… it is *always* only really about *them!*

---

[40] Sperry, L. (2003). *Handbook of Diagnosis and Treatment of DSM-IV-TR Personality Disorders.* (2nd Ed). Brunner- Routledge: New York.

Further Reading:

Lasswell, H. D. (1960). *Psychopathology and Politics*. New York.

Owen, D. (2008). *In Sickness and in Power: Illness in the Heads of Government during the last 100 Years*. Methuen. London.

IMPOSTURE

I is for **Imposture**

"I thought I was broken. I used to sit behind a desk, wearing this decorated uniform, feeling like a scared, incompetent nine-year-old in a hero's costume. For the life of me I couldn't understand why they kept promoting me." [41] US Pentagon Army Colonel

You might find it surprising that the Imposter Syndrome or Imposter Phenomena occurs most commonly in successful and high-achieving individuals. Sufferers of Imposter Syndrome often appear from the outside to have done well, but their success and achievements aren't usually felt fully and authentically within themselves. They are usually too busy making sure *nobody finds them out!* They believe, earnestly, that their successes and achievements are

---

[41] Mount, P., & Tardanico, S. (2014). *Beating the Imposter Syndrome*. Centre for Creative Leadership.

only attained as a fluke; they were in the right place at the right time, they had a lucky break, they knew someone key or they simply worked inordinately hard just to make the grade. Rarely do they accept that their success and achievements are as a direct result of their own talent or intelligence.

Individuals suffering from imposture can experience huge levels of worry and self-doubt. They worry about future failures and doubt they can repeat past performances. They worry about what they don't know and doubt they know enough. They worry about meeting other's expectations and fundamentally doubt they are good enough. Overall, they constantly worry if today is indeed the day they are *going to be found out?* With this doubt and worry comes fear and anxiety. Sometimes this leads to procrastination sometimes to overwork. Although they can appear self-assured and self-confident, they are just disguising what they believe to be their inadequacies and weaknesses and this mask just adds to their feelings of dissatisfaction, insecurity and inauthenticity. They seldom let themselves feel comfortable and confident and rarely let themselves enjoy the sense of satisfaction and accomplishment that should come with their success. In *Leaders, Fools and Imposters* [42] Manfred Kets de Vries describes this phenomenon,

"Imposters are those individuals who feel fraudulent and imposturous while actually being successful. These people have an abiding feeling that they have fooled everyone and are not as competent and intelligent as others think they are. They attribute their success to luck or compensatory hard work. Some are incredibly hardworking, always overprepared. However, they are unable to accept that they have intellectual gifts and ability. They live in constant fear that their imposturous existence will be exposed – that they will not be able to measure up to others' expectations and that catastrophe will follow" (p.129).

The roots of Imposter Syndrome, like much other personal psychology, reach back into childhood when the sufferer did not feel accepted for who they were. They may have felt they experienced only conditional love and approval that required them to live up to their parent's expectations of them, usually around being the best and the smartest. Critical and perfectionist family messages are absorbed, and the

---

[42] Kets de Vries, M. (1993). *Leaders, Fools and Imposters: Essays on the Psychology of Leadership*. Jossey Bass, California.

child carries these messages over with them into their adult working life. Then when praise is received for a piece of work the person can only think of how many mistakes they made and how much better it could and should have been. Ironically, this syndrome can also develop as a result of receiving the opposite form of praise and recognition. A child may have been told that they are gifted and brilliant and can do anything they set their mind to, which also creates a burden to carry into adult life. A burdensome feeling that they should be able to do everything and anything they choose and do it well. As a result, they can feel an intense pressure to achieve in all aspects of their life. These individuals then come in for an unpleasant and uncomfortable ride when they enter the wider world and realise, they aren't the No1 they were always told they were. In this way, conditional love and approval can leave a child damned if they do and damned if they don't. On top of all of this, the parents consciously or unconsciously transmit to their children their own values, opinions, hopes and fears which means they communicate to the child, overtly and covertly, who and what they want them to become. The developing child who knows no better can only absorb these messages whether they fit with their own growing sense-of-self or not. And so, a sense of inauthentic imposture begins.

Later in life, even after the parents are long gone, this fear and threat to self-esteem remains and manifests itself in a variety of ways. For example, imposture individuals are unable to believe compliments from others about their talent or intellect, regardless of any supporting objective evidence. They can become quite creative in the ways they are able to dismiss such feedback. To the extent that they can even convince themselves that success at recruitment or promotion, only comes because the panel themselves are misguided, mistaken or easily fooled – all of which ironically reinforces their sense of fraudulence and inauthenticity. In spite of everything, though, and somewhat paradoxically, these individuals desperately want to know that they are clever and competent, if not outstanding and brilliant. And so, they will develop whatever strategies it takes to continually pull success from the jaws of defeat. Typical strategies can include a heady and oppositional mix of; overwork, avoidance, frantic work pace, procrastination, over-preparation and perfectionism. Individuals come to believe that worry, doubt, panic and anxiety are all necessary ingredients to success. This in turn reinforces the whole cycle, which goes something like:

Doubt/Fear/Anxiety >
Procrastination/Overpreparation > Frenzied Work >
Success > Praise > Relief

In the books *If I'm so successful, why do I feel like a fake* [43] and *Imposter Phenomena* [44] Joan Harvey and Pauline Clance respectively both offer questionnaires designed to assess feelings of Imposter Syndrome. These sets of questions can help individuals explore and begin to understand any imposter feelings they may be experiencing. The scales include some penetrating questions. How might you react to some of their statements, e.g. *In general people tend to believe I am more competent than I am; I find it easy to accept compliments about my competence; I feel I deserve whatever honours, recognition or praise I receive; At times, I have felt I am in my present position through some kind of mistake; I can give the impression that I am more competent than I really am; I avoid evaluations if possible and have a dread of others evaluating me; When people praise me for something I've accomplished, I'm afraid I won't be able to live up to their expectations of me in the future; I'm afraid people important to*

---

[43] Harvey, J., & Katz, C. (1985) *If I'm So Successful, Why Do I Feel Like a Fake?* Pocket Books. New York.

[44] Clance, P. R. (1985). *Imposter Phenomena: Overcoming the Fear that Haunts your Success.* Peachtree. Atlanta, US.

me may find out that I'm not as capable as they think I am; At times, I feel my success has been due to some kind of luck.

If some of these statements do indeed resonate, you will no doubt be wondering what you can do about it? Well, there lies a wealth of material and literature behind each bite-sized chapter in this book and this one is no exception. So, the reader who thinks this is a particular area of interest is pointed in the direction of the reading below as a first step. Needless to say, the topics you will be advised to explore will be around; perfectionist tendencies, fear of evaluation, denial of competence, fear of failure and somewhat intriguingly, fear of success!

Some exploratory questions you may find helpful to ponder ahead of this are; who was the brightest in your family? On what criteria was that based? How was intelligence defined? What was your family's attitude towards intelligence? What was the family narrative about you as a child? What did you feel these stories conveyed about you and the attributes the family considered important? Having reflected on this, what impact do you think it has on your leadership? How and where does it manifest that is most significant for you?

J is for **Jung**

"Everything with substance casts a shadow." [45] Carl Jung

Carl Jung was a contemporary of Freud and from his many important ideas, one that I think is particularly germane to our exploration of authenticity is his idea of the Shadow. He introduces it to us through one of his dreams,

"I had a dream which both frightened me and encouraged me. It was night in some unknown place, and I was making slow progress and painful headway against a mighty wind. Dense fog was flowing along everywhere. I

---

[45] Zweig, C. & Abrams, J. (Eds) (1991). *Meeting the Shadow*. Penguin. New York.

had my hands cupped around a tiny light which threatened to go out at any moment. Everything depended on my keeping this little light alive. Suddenly I had the feeling that someone was coming up behind me. I looked back, and saw a gigantic black figure following me. But at the same moment I was conscious, in spite of my terror, that I must keep my little light going through night and wind, regardless of all dangers. When I awoke, I realised at once that the figure was my own shadow on the swirling mists, brought into being by the little light I was carrying. I knew, too, that this little light was my consciousness" [46] (p.24).

So, the light is our consciousness and the shadow is our unconscious. In the shadow dwells all of our qualities and characteristics that we're forced to hide away while growing up in what has been called the psychic-soup of our family environments. This all happens long before we can rationalise cause and effect or think abstractly about our family relations and interrelations. When all we can do when the need is pressed upon us, is to squash down the unwelcome parts of ourselves somewhere out of the way - out into the shadow. When we upset, angered or disappointed our caregivers and we couldn't grasp

---

[46] Monbourquette, J. (2001). *How to Befriend your Shadow*. Novalis. Canada.

why, the only real option was for us to supress the emotions, behaviours, qualities or characteristics in question so we wouldn't risk losing their affection and approval. In this psychic-soup we are exposed to a swirl of familial behaviours, expectations, norms and dysfunctions including our parent's own unresolved issues that no doubt influenced their own parenting style or coping patterns. In amongst all this drama and over time, when we have no sophisticated coping strategies ourselves, more and more pieces of our natural self are moved off into the shadow. Pieces that just don't fit the picture of who we are learning we need to become. The neglected, the rejected and the unacceptable pieces are relegated elsewhere, in effect creating a whole shadowy underground part of ourselves. However, this is not a quiet dormant underground. Repressing pieces of ourselves does not eliminate them, it merely puts them out of our awareness. But removed from awareness also means removed from direct supervision and this can become problematic, as what lives in the shadow is still very much alive, active and demanding expression. Until such time as we can re-own what lives in our shadow the only way it can find such expression is by us externally projecting it out into the world, which can create an unholy mess as it distorts our perception of reality by attributing to others what we fail to recognise or accept in ourselves.

We have already met this phenomenon recently in discussing Hitler. His fear and hatred were all his own but when he came to power, he was able to rationalise and externalise them by projecting them outwards onto his many imaginary enemies. Donald Trump, who we meet in greater detail later, is a very vivid and startling modern-day lesson in projection. In his mind his enemies are legion; the Fake Media, the Deep State, the Democrats, Nancy Pelosi, Barack Obama, Hilary Clinton, China, Korea, the EU, NATO, WHO. Eventually every single individual he has to deal with, be they his own Military, Intelligence or fellow politicians, will become a target for his projections. And tellingly, everything he accuses them of doing or being, he is plainly guilty of himself. He will attribute (and believe!) dishonesty, ignorance, weakness, criminality, incompetence and nepotism to all of his adversaries, while seemingly unaware himself what everyone else watching clearly sees – that these are all fundamental characteristics in himself. Such is the power of projection. Just like a real shadow that follows us, others can often notice it long before we do. This is aptly described in *Meeting the Shadow* [47],

> "Ask someone to give a description of the personality type which he finds most unbearable and most impossible to get along with, and he will produce a description of his own repressed characteristics – a self-description which is utterly unconscious" (p.14).

Ironically, in a self-reflecting and self-fulfilling prophecy, the person projecting then becomes the victim of their own projections as they become haunted or threatened by their own shadow reflecting back at them – "*Like the boxer who trains by fighting his own shadow, the shadow projector is condemned to this exhausting, never-ending exercise in shadow boxing*" [48] (p.16). Hitler shadow boxed right up until his death and it's almost inevitable that Donald Trump will do the same.

There are different options of how to deal with our shadow. One way is to refuse to face it, deny it, and let it have its own way, which it will. However, this strategy merely relegates its energy to the unconscious

---

[47] Zweig, C. & Abrams, J. (Eds) (1991). *Meeting the Shadow*. Penguin. New York.

[48] Monbourquette, J. (2001). *How to Befriend your Shadow*. Novalis. Canada.

from where it "… *exerts its power in a negative, compulsive, projected form*" (p.17) as it does quite clearly with Trump "*Then our projections will transform our surrounding world into a setting which shows us our own faces, though we do not recognise them as our own*" (p.17). Here we can become isolated with just an illusory relationship with our outside world. A world where our projections eventually shape our attitudes towards others and bring about that which we project, which again in the case of Trump is fear, hostility and isolation, "*We imagine ourselves so long pursued by ill will that ill will is eventually produced by others in response to our vitriolic defensiveness*" (p.17).

However, by confronting our shadow we can have some element of control over when, where and how it expresses its tendencies. But the first step is to acknowledge its presence. Despite its elusive and mysterious nature, and its ability to hide in our unconscious, we have to accept that it exists and lives as an integral part of our personality. The shadows independent patterns of thought and emotion retain a life and energy of their own which means they cannot be stopped or changed simply by an act of will. Becoming aware of our shadow and owning it is the door to a more full and integrated sense of authentic self. Some even suggest that there is no other access to our unconscious or to a full authentic personal reality than through this door. So, the aim is not to eliminate or banish your shadow, it is to understand, accept and integrate it. When you start to integrate your shadow, you become a lot more realistic about yourself and see the truth about your own genuine nature. But beginning this path of self-enquiry has to start with brutal honesty. Ask yourself what is it about a particular individual, or group of individuals, that irritates, annoys or otherwise repels you? If something of this person or group simply informs, then you are probably not projecting. If, however, something affects you to such a degree that you react strongly and emotionally, then you are probably projecting something of your own shadow onto them. This seemingly simple exploration can lead, further down the road, to a whole new world of understanding, acceptance and even compassion for both others, and yourself. It will ultimately help you live with less self-deception and self-delusion with more balanced thinking and decision making. It is not always easy, as we will try and convince ourselves, despite the evidence, other people or groups are indeed exactly as we have judged them. But as Jung says about such shadow work *"long and difficult negotiations will be unavoidable"* (p.271). Individual shadows are both universal and inevitable and only really become pathological when we deny we have one. Because, if, we assume we don't have *it,* then *it* has *us*! And as Jung would say - *it will have its way and we will call that fate.*

So, accepting that we all have a shadow side, the key questions to consider are; what's in yours and how does it express itself? Who are the people you really struggle to work with? Why do you think that is? Can you see anything of your own dark side in them? Finally, and this may seem a bit strange, but ask your shadow what it needs from you? Remember it is not there to purposively create conflict – but it *does* need expression so it will help you to know what it seeks through that expression. Ultimately, these are the kind of questions that will help you illuminate your shadow so you can see it more clearly and eventually understand it and integrate it.

Further Reading:

Jung, C. G. (1991). *The Archetypes and the Collective Unconscious.* Routledge. UK.

Jung, C. G. (1995). *Memories, Dreams, Reflections.* Fontana Press. US.

Strorr, A. (2013). *The Essential Jung.* Fontana Press. US.

K is for **Kierkegaard**

"The thing is to find a truth that is true for me, to find the idea for which I can live and die." [49]

The Dutch philosopher Soren Kierkegaard (1813-1855) is generally considered the founder of Existential Philosophy introduced earlier. He was a deeply melancholic man and took his anguish as the starting point for a journey of deep self-discovery. He sought the truth about himself personally and the human condition generally. He was among the first to develop in any meaningful way the key existential

---

[49] Kierkegaard, S., & Hannay, A. (2005). *Fear and Trembling*. Penguin. UK.

themes, such as the absurdity of life, the weight and importance of individual choice and responsibility, and the need to live an authentic life. What makes him one of the undisputed founders of Existentialism was the way he rejected the systematic answers of both traditional philosophy and orthodox religion and made philosophy deeply personal. He believed the big questions had meaning only in the way they were lived out by each person. He argued that abstract philosophic reason or generic religious commandments couldn't really answer the question of how you should live personally, but these concrete questions had to be asked and answered in the depths of each individual's soul.

Kierkegaard focussed most of his work on the psychology and philosophy of Ethics, Morality and Religion. He was a great thinker but one who applied his philosophy directly to a way of life, believing that the creation of an authentic life was nothing short of an existential vocation. As such his overriding concern was with personal choice and commitment in how to live one's life as an individual *"The thing is to find a truth that is true for me, to find the idea for which I can live and die"* (p15). Kierkegaard was deeply influenced by Socrates and praised the Grecian for being the first to study with decisive force the concept of the existing individual and you can hear him in lines such as *"One must first learn to know himself before knowing anything else"*. As well as thought, there was also an influence on style. Much like Socrates, Kierkegaard wasn't prone to direct instruction or lecturing. He preferred a more indirect form of communicating allowing people to learn their own lessons through his descriptions of his own personal life views. Often not concluding anything at all rather just illuminating all sides of the prism, in much the same way that Socrates did by using questioning as his primary tool of enquiry.

Kierkegaard believed that living authentically was to live an intense and deliberate life, to confront and grapple with the serious business of life with its own individual significance and meaning. He believed we should find a meaning and a cause for our own life and, if it isn't something we are prepared to die for, it should certainly be something we are prepared to live for. Something to commit to, organise our lives around and embody. As individuals responsible for ourselves I think this is imperative. For senior leaders responsible for others, possibly even more so.

Even in the mid 19th century, Kierkegaard observed that most people just wanted a safe and easy life and were happy for life answers to be handed down to them, thus avoiding the anxiety and angst of their own personal wrestle with life. He urged us to find our own existential calling – to stake out our own lives. The very integrity of our life depends on it and it's what our life demands of us. This requires choosing a direction for your life that expresses your own individual nature from within and not from without. Finding this personal truth for Kierkegaard was key. But he differentiated objective truth from subjective truth; one pertains to the existence of objects and the other of subjects. Science prizes the quest for object truth, whereas existential phenomenology holds dear the quest for subjective truth. If I find my subjective truth, that is, an idea or ideal worth living (and dying) for, science cannot tell me that this is either right or wrong, nor can the cosmos, nor can my family, friends or colleagues – ultimately only I can judge. This, Kierkegaard called the difference between the *Approximation* versus the *Appropriation* of truth.

Approximation of the truth basically involves the scientific method. This means you look at all data and the rational reasons for choosing a particular truth to live by; an idea, ideal, cause, path, direction etc. You weigh the evidence and conclude that, on balance, the odds are in favour of this being a truth you can confidently and comfortably choose. But this means your chosen truth actually comes from outside of you. It's an objective reality open for all to consider and assess. It comes from the public domain and not the personal realm. It offers assurance from the outside that your choices are the right ones and that your truth is a valid one. Approximation, Kierkegaard believed, was fine for answering questions about the nature of objects but not questions about the existence of subjects. Appropriation, on the other hand, he believed more relevant in choosing the personal truth you want to live your life by. Rather than seeking outside evidence for your truth, you have to believe in it from the inside. The motivation and commitment to it has to be understood and owned in a deeply personal way. Appropriation of a personal truth, that cannot be fully underwritten by objective proof or evidence, means moving beyond a comfortable, easy life. It means walking an uncertain path but one that shapes who and what you are, and one that Kierkegaard believes is the embodiment of an authentic life.

This question of choosing independently a path, goal or vocation is one the existentialists never tire of, and rightly so. It takes considerable effort (and courage) to just confront such questions – let alone answer and act on them. Do any such questions occupy any of your time? If they do, where does that path of enquiry take you? If they don't, is that OK with you? Sometimes sleeping dogs are at their happiest in their slumber. Sometimes, they simply slumber while they wait…

Further Reading:

Dru. A. (1938). *The Journals of Soren Kierkegaard*. Ed and trans. London. Oxford University Press.

Ferguson, R. (2013). *Life Lessons from Kierkegaard*. Macmillan. London.

Gardiner, P. (1988). *Kierkegaard: A Very Short Introduction*. Oxford University Press. Oxford.

Kierkegaard, S., & Hong, H. V. (2000). *The Essential Kierkegaard*. Princeton University Press. UK.

Logistical **LEADERSHIP**

L is for **Logistical Leadership**

"The natural thing to do is work. For the days' work is a great thing – a very great thing! It is at the very foundation of the world and the basis of our self-respect." [50] Henry Ford

For the Logistical leader it is both easy and enjoyable to practice and develop their logistical skills. Logistics is the efficient and effective procurement and distribution of material goods and is vital to the success of any institution be it a business, school or army. Such leaders can be enormously creative in seeing to it that the right personnel have the right supplies in the right place at the right time to get the job done. They care about being reliable, particularly in the maintenance and continuity of their organisations. Therefore, they may be less interested in fitting things together in a new way than in holding

---

[50] Ford, H. (2018). *My Life and Work: Henry Ford Autobiography.* In Collaboration with Samuel Crowther. US.

things together as they are. Logistical leaders know that change is inevitable and often necessary, however, they find change unsettling and so they may resist it if it comes at the expense of time-tested ways that have served the institution well thus far. They are both interested in and excel at occupations that have to do with the logistical management of material and as such the most talented often become managers, executives and leading business figures and include within their ranks industry giants such as; J.D. Rockefeller, J.P. Getty, J.P. Morgan, H.J. Heinz, J.C. Penny and F.W. Woolworth.

The Logistical leader believes that the key to honour (and assets) is a respect for law, order, authority, tradition, caution and a persistent attention to one's resources. As such they are highly skilled in accumulating and preserving materials and seeing to it that authorised personnel receive those resources at the authorised time and place and excel at the collection, storage and distribution of materials to those sanctioned to receive it. More broadly it is their job to make sure that people do what they are supposed to do, what their duty calls upon them to do. As a result, the Logistical leader quickly takes notes of the transgressions of others, whether they be errors of omission or commission. As they are less likely to remember when others do what they *should* do, they are quite likely to be unforgiving when others do what they should *not* do. Of each of the four leadership temperaments that we meet throughout the alphabet, the Logistical leader will be the one most concerned and preoccupied with matters of preservation, duty, reward and punishment. After all, sanctioned cooperation is the very foundation of an effective and civilised society or organisation. These leaders have a deep and abiding sense of responsibility to any group they belong to. Whatever the group is, if they are connected to it, they are bound to preserve and protect it, and this means duty, obligation and loyalty, which they take very seriously. Nor would they have it any other way – they seek obligation which they relish and even flourish under its often, heavy weight. The Logistical leader also prefers concreteness of expression. They can be impatient with 'as-ifs' and 'what-ifs' and with ideas and theories which are merely imaginary rather than down-to-earth and sensible. Their leadership is predominantly orientated towards the preservation of the organisation's rules, traditions and protocols. They can bring enormous effort and determination to their leadership along with impressive moral stature and unswerving loyalty.

The leadership case study for this temperament is the

American captain of industry and business magnate Henry Ford (1863-1947), founder of the Ford Motor Company and pioneer of the assembly line method of mass production.

Henry Ford embodies the sense of duty and service encapsulated above. He believed machinery, money and goods were useful as they set one free to live. He believed ideas themselves valuable, but that an idea is just an idea, and almost anyone can think up an idea. The thing that counts is developing it into a practical product. He would say that the foundations of society are the men and means to make things as these help the world survive economic and social change. Though Ford believed that money was necessary, he also believed that what came after wealth should not be a life of ease, but the opportunity to perform ever more service. There is no place in civilisation for the idler. In his factories he considered waste and greed to be the two keys blocks to providing that service. Waste he said, is largely due to not understanding what you are doing or being careless in doing it and that greed was merely a form of near-sightedness. He sums his whole business philosophy up in true Logistical leader fashion – *"I have strived towards manufacturing with a minimum of waste, both of materials and of human effort, and then towards distribution at a minimum of profit, depending for the total profit upon the volume of distribution*". He goes on to say, "*In the process of manufacturing I want to distribute the maximum of wage and the maximum of buying power. Thus, everyone who is connected with us – either as a manager, worker or purchaser – is the better for our existence. Then this institution that we have built is performing a service.*"

This inextricable link between money, manufacture and service helped Henry Ford become one of history's wealthiest men amassing a fortune of around $200bn. But key to his whole philosophy was that finance came second to service, right from the beginning.

"The year from 1902 until the formation of the Ford Motor Company was practically one of investigation. I tried to find out what business really was and whether it needed to be quite so selfish a scramble for money as it seemed to be from my first short experience. The most surprising feature of business as it was conducted was the large attention given to finance and the small attention given to service. This seemed to me to be reversing the natural process which is that the money should come as the result of work and not before the work. I determined absolutely that never would I build a company in which finance came before the work. For the only foundation of real business is service. When one serves for the sake of service – for the satisfaction of doing that which one believes to be right – then money takes care of itself. As we serve our jobs, so we serve the world."

Throughout his career, Ford continued to strive for good wages for his employees and good prices for his customers. This is what drove both his organisational design and his assembly line design: *"It is not good management to take profits out of the workers or the buyers, make management produce the profits. Don't cheapen the product, don't cheapen the wage, don't overcharge the public. Put brains into the method, more brains and still more brains. Do things better than ever before and by this means all parties to business are served and benefitted."*

Ford also applied his principles of duty, loyalty, obligation and service to staff wages, working capital and profit. Of wages he said,

"People ought to tread very carefully when approaching wages, there is something sacred about them - they represent homes and families and domestic destinies. On the cost sheet, wages are mere figures but out in the world, wages are bread boxes and coal bins, babies' cradles and children's education."

He believed equally in the sanctity of working capital and profit. On profit he said,

"Profit belongs in three places: it should go to provide a sounder basis for the business, better working conditions, better wages and more extended employment. As such, the profits belong to the business – to keep it steady, progressive and sound. They belong to the men who helped produce them. And they belong also, in part, to the public."

Finally, his views on capital were that,

"There is something just as sacred about capital which is used to provide the means by which work can be made more productive. If capital is not constantly creating more and better jobs it is useless. Capital that is not making conditions of daily labour better and the reward more just, is not fulfilling its highest function. The highest use of capital is not to make more money, but to make money do more service for the betterment of life. Thus, capital may be under the direction of one, but it is for the service of all."

These were the core principles behind Ford's famous democratisation of the motor car. He held that it was better to sell a large number of cars at a reasonably small margin than to sell fewer cars at a large margin of profit. He took this view because it enabled a large number of people to buy and enjoy the use of a car and because it gave a larger number of workers employment at good wages. *"Those are aims I have in life"* he said. And his policy worked. Since the factory was returned to automobile production after the WW1 war effort, with each succeeding year he was able to put his car within the reach of greater and greater numbers, give employment to more and more men and, at the same time, through the volume of the business, increase his profits beyond anything he hoped or dreamed when he started.

How about you? Are you in your element losing yourself in amongst the organisational cogs and mechanisms? Working out how all the different connections flow and work together feeding in and off each other? How to make them more stable and more efficient? If your 'leadership home' is in the established here-and-now it will influence all around you – for better and for worse. So, be the vigilant, loyal, responsible guardian-leader you are... just ensure you have a team around you who are also doing the more abstract but still necessary creative and future-orientated work!

MEANING

M is for **Meaning**

"The question of life's meaning is the most urgent question of all." [51]
Albert Camus

We humans are meaning-making creatures. Our brains are so complex and restless that we simply can't help ourselves. Anthropologists estimate that around 97% of the human population has some form of religious, spiritual or superstitious belief and it can be reasonably argued that all of this is simply an attempt to find or make meaning of the world and our place within it. Such beliefs, in all their guises can offer Man unparalleled sources of meaning for life. They can provide not just a reason for our present life, but even a route to and reason for the next. Such beliefs offer us answers as to where we came from, where we are going and even the right path to take to

---

[51] Camus, A. (1981). *The Myth of Sisyphus* in *The Meaning of Life*. E.D Klemke (Ed.) Oxford University Press. UK.

get there. All of which are substantial answers to meaning-related questions that can be neatly handed to us directly from almost any form of faith or religion on offer. But superstitious or religious beliefs are not our only source of meaning, there is of course also; family, career, nature, art, sport, science, health, wealth or wisdom, wherever it is we personally find it. The point is that we are incurable in our quest for it. We want things to have form and order and so look for reason and rationale in almost everything we see and experience.

The irony, however, is that in existential terms - there simply is no form or order or meaning and this is what a philosopher means when they talk about *absurdity* – the fact that we crave and seek meaning where there is none. Evolution has endowed us with brains able to conjure up the ideas of ghosts and gods, create elaborate religions and philosophies, build castles and cathedrals and yet despite all this, we return in the end to the earth to feed the worms! Understandably, we find this immensely disturbing and difficult to comprehend and so rather than live with such absurdity we create elaborate alternatives, both for this world and the next. The Universe, however, is quite unconcerned with our health, happiness or peace of mind and simply incubates our existence in a quite indifferent way and so throws us back onto ourselves to find our own meaning. At first this might seem somewhat depressing, but when you think carefully about it, it is also very liberating. If the world is not inherently under-written with meaning passed over to us, then we are free to seek our own. Indeed, as we have seen, existentialists argue we actually have a responsibility to seek it and create it. To make conscious choices that are significant and important to us, so that we can lead a meaningful and authentic life. But let's pause for a moment and ask - what does meaning actually mean?

The existential view is that life doesn't come with pre-packed and preordained meaning. This is not to say that we don't or can't have meaningful lives, just that our meaning has to be personally constructed by each of us. Whatever source of meaning we chose, faith, career, service, charity etc, we have to do so actively and not passively. We shouldn't wait for meaning to be assigned to us from on high. But even though we must actively determine the meaning of our own life, we also have to accept that meanings may still have to be chosen from those 'on offer' from within our own culture, community, era and circumstance. Many cultures typically offer their own off-the-shelf sets of meanings in the form of norms and values, and many people readily accept these without much thought or consideration and still manage to build on them a meaningful life. Community tradition, societal custom, religious systems or political structures all offer both meaning and comfort in that they give us a shared past and future and even a direction of travel between the two, telling us how to think and act on the journey, thereby affording us a sometimes profound sense of both meaning and belonging.

But how do we actually define meaning? One proposition is that meaning connects things and is a "... *shared mental representation of possible relationships among things, events and relationships*" [52] (p.12). Another is that meaning is about "... *having the parts fit together into a coherent pattern, being capable of being understood by others, fitting into a broader context*" (p.16) the opposite being "... *disconnected chaos, internal contradiction, or failure to fit...*" (p.16). These definitions allude to the important point that meaning can have multiple levels, based on increasingly complex interrelations and even time perspectives. For example, at a low and immediate level you are simply getting on the train to go to a football match with your son. But considered from a

---

[52] Baumeister, R. (1991). *Meanings of Life*. The Guildford Press. New York.

higher and longer perspective, this simple act invokes much richer meanings that may revolve around family ties, community tradition, social camaraderie and belongingness. Individual acts are therefore infused with significance and purpose when they feed up into a more broad, integrated and coherent whole. Meaning is thus more likely to flow downwards than upwards. For example, the lower-level immediate questions about getting to the football match relates to the *how*. Whereas the higher-level longer-term issues and questions, will all relate to the *why?* So, meaning is about constructing broad, integrated interpretations. They are less about the *how* and more about the *why*.

Even at a cultural level such as an ideology, these systems can be thought of as a set of cultural meanings that tell people how to interpret events and make value judgements. Even though such ideological systems are not necessarily logical systems per se, they can be powerful psychological systems, which may help explain their appeal and endurance. They can offer a basic set of attitudes that help people quickly assess and understand things as either good or bad or right or wrong. They also help people move from the higher levels of meaning to the lower levels to explain specific acts or events i.e. why did that earthquake wipe out our entire town, why did the rain destroy our crops, why do we suffer hardship or injustice? Because of our behaviour, our disobedience, or any number of other ways we may have displeased the gods of harvest, fertility, prosperity etc.

In *Meanings of Life* [53] Roy Baumeister believed he identified four broad ways in which people typically find meaning in their lives, through; *purpose, value, self-efficacy* and *self-worth*. Regarding purpose Baumeister says that we have to see our activities orientated towards a purpose. Such purpose does not even have to be realised or achieved as it is quite possible to live a meaningful life in pursuit of goals that are never actually reached during our lifetime. He cites the example of the patriotic soldier who dies defending his country and that we wouldn't think he lived a meaningless life simply because the war was not won while he was alive. A second category of Baumeister's meaning is the need for feeling life has some form of value and that our actions are right, good and justifiable and that we need to see our current actions and lives as having a positive value. A third source of meaning is through a sense of self-efficacy, the need

---

[53] Baumeister, R. (1991). *Meanings of Life*. The Guildford Press. New York.

to believe that we have some sense of control over events in our life and the need to feel that we're making a difference of some sort. Having a meaningful life is more than having goals and values, we must also feel that we have some capability to achieve these goals and realise these values. His fourth and final need for meaning comes from a need for self-worth and our need to find some basis for positive self-regard. We more often than not seek some criteria according to which we can think of ourselves positively. We have a need for respect, both of self-respect and respect from others.

As we then see, the issue of meaning for humans can be a complex one. We have an innate need to make sense of the things, to order them, categorise and connect them. We much prefer to create an overall pattern of things than to have them remain random, isolated and unconnected. This makes the world, and our lives within it, stable, predictable and controllable. When we face a dislocated and indifferent world, we feel tense, dissatisfied, even helpless and so we inevitably begin to piece together patterns, explanations and meanings, which returns to us a comfortable sense of certainty and mastery. Importantly though, having meaning is not necessarily the same as being happy. It often trumps happiness.

You can be satisfied that you have a meaningful life even if it's not a happy life - think again of a suffering soldier or an aid worker bringing emergency relief to a disaster zone, neither may be described as happy yet both live lives infused with a sense of meaning. However, it's hard to imagine a happy and satisfying life that is totally devoid of all sense of meaning. What happens in such circumstances? Great thinkers and writers have long grappled with this question. For the existential French novelist Albert Camus, it was the philosophical question at the heart of everything, *"I have seen many die because life for them was not worth living. From this I conclude that the question of life's meaning is the most urgent question of all"* [54]. Even the legendary Russian novelist Leo Tolstoy grappled with the issue during a crisis that he called his life's arrest, *"The question... was the simplest of all questions, lying in the soul of everyman – what will become of what I am doing now, and may do tomorrow. What will come from my whole life? Why should I live?"* [55].

In the more contemporary *The Meaning of Life* [56] John

---

[54] Camus, A. (1981). *The Myth of Sisyphus* in *The Meaning of Life*. E.D Klemke (Ed.) Oxford University Press. UK.

[55] Tolstoy, L. (1887). *Confessions*. (D. Patterson, Trans.).

[56] Messerly, J. (2012). *The Meaning of Life: Religious, Philosophical, Transhumanist and Scientific Perspectives*. (Amazon. GB.)

Messerly makes the point *"In the end, the question of the meaning of life dissolves into or reduces to the question of how we should live"* (p.67). So, perhaps all along we've been asking the wrong question. One that becomes more meaningful itself with the simple change of one little word. Rather than asking about the meaning *of* life perhaps we should be asking about the meaning *in* life? In his book Messerly quotes from David Schmidt who lists what he personally believes to be the components of a meaningful life. Schmidt suggests that meanings are symbolic and that something may be meaningful to one person, not to another and vice versa. A straightforward example might help illustrate this in the form of a simple cornfield. The most obvious purpose, or meaning, of such a thing would be the food it produces for the consumer and the livelihood it produces for the farmer. But what about the artist who chooses to reproduce it on canvass? The children who play in it or the lovers who hide in it? What about the light aircraft pilot who circles above using it to read wind direction as he prepares to land? And, so it goes on. The field of corn objectively exists but its meaning can be said to be subjectively constructed. Schmidt proposes that meanings are choices. He argues with crushing logic, *"We choose whether our lives have sufficient meaning for us. If we choose to view them as meaningless, then we should not worry about it since that is meaningless too. And if we can't enjoy meaninglessness, then we should choose to treat life as meaningful*' (p.144).

Philosopher Robert Solomon poses some interesting and challenging questions. First to those who would say family and in particular having children is what gives their life meaning. But what then, Solomon asks, is the meaning of your children's life? And their children's? He extends this challenge to those who believe religion gives their life meaning. Here, he thinks we need to ask the question 'Why did God/s create us - for what purpose?' If it was for some purpose, then what was it? Why do they need us? If they did create us for some purpose how does their purpose make my life meaningful – it is *their* purpose and not *mine*, after all? Very similar questions arise about another of religions great promises – the afterlife. Is our existing life so without significance that only the promise of a new and different one can inject our current one with meaning? And an everlasting afterlife just compounds matters. How on earth do you make an eternal afterlife meaningful? Solomon argues that the meaning of a life does not have a specific and objective answer. Rather, like Schmidt's idea of a subject's symbolic meanings, he believes it comes down to the vision we have of our life. He goes as far as to offer us some alternatives as to how we can envision meaning in our lives, among them we can see our lives as a game, a story, a tragedy, a mission, or as art, adventure, honour, learning or relationship. How might you consider your life, as a;

- Game – though you might not take it too seriously, do you still want to win or be a good sport?
- Story – do you see yourself as the hero of an unfolding narrative or drama?
- Tragedy – do you feel you must live a brave and dignified life even in the face of adversity and suffering?
- Mission – do you seek to convert others, promote justice, science or revolution?
- Art – are you given over to the creation of beauty?
- Adventure – do you seek a life lived to the full along with all its risks and challenges?
- Honour – is it one in which you must fulfil all expectations of you and do your duty?
- Learning – must you grow and develop and fulfil all of your potential?
- Relationship – is life about love, family and friendship at the centre of all?

Each of these represent different ways to envision your life. In so doing, you may still not find the answer to the meaning *of* your life, but you may well find the answer to the authentic meaning *in* your life.

In terms of leadership, you might want to consider: what is it that you believe is the fundamental *purpose* of your leadership? How is this characterised or informed by your own personal *values?* Do you feel competent and *efficacious* in carrying out this leadership task and mission? If yes or no, how does this impact your own sense of *self-worth*. What conclusions do you derive from this enquiry? These are not inconsequential questions to ponder.

Further Reading:

Baggini, J. (2004). *What's it all about? Philosophy and the Meaning of Life.* Granta Books. London.

Cottingham, J. (2003). *On the Meaning of Life.* Thinking in Action. Routledge. Oxon. UK.

Crumbaugh & Maholick. (1964). *Purpose in Life Test.*

Durrant. W. (2001). *On the Meaning of Life.* Promethean Press. Carrolton: US.

Ford, D. (2007). *The Search for Meaning: A Short History.* University of California Press. Berkeley. US.

Grayling, A. C. (2003). *The Meanings of Things: Applying Philosophy to Life*. Phoenix. London.

N is for **Nietzsche**

"Where has God gone? I shall tell you. We have killed him – you and I, we are his murderers. What did we do when we unchained the earth from its sun?" [57] Friedreich Nietzsche

For many, Friedreich Nietzsche (1844-1900) is the second father of Existentialism and gave us its greatest challenge when he proclaimed - *God is dead!* And, if he is, then so too is the greatest system of thought that Man ever created to make sense of and give meaning to the world. If God is dead, so too is the sense of meaning, order and purpose that we all need to protect ourselves from the anxiety we feel

---

[57] Nietzsche, F. (1954). *Thus Spoke Zarathustra* (Trans.) W. Kaufmann. Viking. New York.

when we have to confront our unadorned existence. This honest comprehension of existence first leads to feelings of angst, then absurdity and then authenticity. Angst that life is not automatically underwritten by some greater purpose or meaning. Absurdity at the sheer randomness of the existence of our life in the vastness of a fundamentally indifferent universe. And authenticity because, if all this is true, you really can become author of your own life and, in Nietzsche's words, *become more of who you already are*. Only after the death of God can you face the meaninglessness of the world and take responsibility for the direction of your own life. Even if the world is inherently meaningless, existentialism asserts that it doesn't have to stay that way, if we take over the responsibility of creating our own meaning in the world.

Nietzsche's proclamation that God is dead meant that the church wasn't at the centre of things anymore. It wasn't at the centre of people's thinking and so no longer underwrote values and meaning for society as a whole. In the religious narrative, God authors our existence and gives it meaning and purpose. God makes the universe an orderly place, everything is valued, everything has purpose, and everything has meaning according to the grand narrative. So, the death of God and religion is a traumatic event as it has historically given people answers as to where they stand, where they fit and what their function is, which makes life comforting and easy. However, this situation also offers tremendous possibilities. When these comforting belief systems are removed, we have to confront our own existence more directly, honestly and authentically. Therefore, if God is dead, life does not become meaningless and insignificant, it simply takes on the meaning and the significance that we choose to give it.

Nietzsche was also a perceptive and relentless social critic demolishing everything he saw as dubious, deluded or damaging to human growth. He believed that only when we have torn down the veil of falsehoods can we really know, enjoy and love the world for what it is on honest terms. He tended to use the term individuality more than authenticity and he believed engaging with the world as an individual was life's most important task and that we should give expression to life through our own unique perspective and purpose. He said that when you achieve this you are in control and you become what you already are. Being an authentic individual means defining yourself and making conscious choices about your life that accurately represent that on-going uniqueness. Nietzsche believed that we are continually in flux and as we are exposed to more life experience we must continually examine and evolve our thoughts and perspectives. He stressed that we must continually reappraise and rethink our understanding of ourselves and our worlds to ensure they remain a true expression of who we authentically are, not to sleepwalk but to move consciously through life. The purpose of this *self-overcoming* as Nietzsche termed it is to achieve maturity, authenticity and profound self-knowledge and to be "...*the free author of one's own self*". Such insights led none other than Sigmund Freud to exclaim, "*He had a more penetrating knowledge of himself than any other man who ever lived or was ever likely to live.*"

Do you sleep-walk or move consciously through your life and your leadership? Do your actions define who you uniquely are? And do you make conscious choices about your life and leadership that accurately represent that uniqueness?

Further Reading:

Nietzsche, F. & Tanner, M. (1992). *Ecce Homo: How One Becomes What One Is*. Penguin. US.

Nietzsche, F. & Kaufmann, W. (1994). *The Portable Nietzsche*. Penguin. US.

ORGANIZATIONAL
DEVELOPMENT

O is for **Organisational Development**

The perennial problem with Organisational and Leadership development has long been to demonstrate a return on investment (ROI). The ROI Institute [58] lists key conditions that need to be satisfied if such development programmes are to be evaluated at the *return on investment* or even the *business impact* level. They say it is crucial to align the programme objectives with the strategic priorities of the organisation which you do by identifying the core skills and knowledge required to achieve these key organisational goals. You then build these into the development programme. Quite straightforward - yet

---

[58] Philips, P. P., Philips, J. P., Stone. R. D., & Burkett, H. Butterworth Heinemann. (2007). *The ROI Field Book: Strategies for Implementing ROI in HR and Training.* Elsevier. Oxford. UK.

rarely done!

Established organisational development orthodoxy is broadly as follows. To ensure leadership development programmes can be properly evaluated you need to develop programme objectives, in particular *application* and *impact* objectives. The purpose of these objectives is to state as clearly as possible what trainees are expected to be able to do at the end of a program. They are usually written from a performance perspective and state how participants should be able to perform in one way or another after the programme is complete and often come with an attached metric such as frequency or quality. The *application* objective defines what the participant is expected to do with what they learn, while the *impact* objective describes what the consequences of this will be. As such, they are highly prescriptive and traditionally have three elements. They not only state what observable behaviour should be demonstrable by the individual after the training, but also to what standard and under what conditions. So, not only are they highly prescriptive, but also to a highly granular level. They are nonetheless traditionally considered useful for the measurement and evaluation of a training programme, inasmuch as they are (or should be) closely linked to the competencies identified in the initial training needs analysis. In essence, such organisational competencies are also standard performance indicators. They can be used as a description of a work task i.e. *what* a person has to do in a job, or as a description of a behaviour i.e. *how* a person is to do that job. Like objectives, competencies traditionally include *performance indicators* that are in turn composed of *behavioural statements*, so once again they operate at a very high level of specificity. Some organisational competence frameworks even go as far as to include all of the above, in that they detail the *task*, the required *behaviours* and the desired *outputs*, even in management and leadership. That is a lot of detail, that some may say falls only slightly short of telling an individual how to put one foot in front of the other!

Whilst all of this may sound like good Learning and Development (L&D) practice, it is problematic for the development of authentic leaders. By its very nature, Authentic Leadership Development (ALD) has to leave it up to the individual to discover what learning and behaviour change needs to happen for them to achieve greater congruence within their role as a leader. It is not for anyone else to tell an individual what it is they need to learn to be more authentic. It will always fall to the individual to discover this for themselves. Genuine ALD should not and does not dictate what a leader must learn, neither can it predict how they will apply what they have learnt and what the impact of that might be. Frustrating for the L&D or accounting professional perhaps, but not necessarily so for the leader concerned. Experienced, motivated professional leaders at all levels are trusted in their roles to develop and lead departments, divisions and entire companies. Why then should they not be trusted to assume control over their own personal development? Even at a senior level, leaders are still often shoehorned into pre-existing competency frameworks of desired traits and behaviours. This is an issue that brings genuine ALD into potential conflict with the orthodoxy of corporate L&D as many organisations want to know exactly what tools and techniques participants will 'pick up' in ALD.

Personally, I think this betrays either a lack of imagination or a chronic lack of ambition for leadership development – or both. The dumbing down of much typical leadership development seems to have led to a situation where many organisations are happy for their leaders to learn more 'tips and tricks' rather than achieve genuine levels of deep and enduring personal transformation that can lead to paradigm shifts in their perspective and performance.

For example, the development of enhanced levels of emotional intelligence and resilience are consistent areas of development in ALD. As are greater levels of strategic awareness and a greater understanding of personal leadership challenges and responsibilities. Such significant learning is not born of tips, tricks, tools or techniques, but fundamental shifts in how individuals see both themselves and their leadership. Therefore, I don't personally believe the competency and objectives treatment is an appropriate one for Authentic Leadership Development, nor do I believe it to be an appropriate one for intelligent, motivated and experienced leaders. A competency-based leadership development programme is simply not a leader-centric one. By definition, such an approach prioritises one particular leadership model or behaviour as best-in-class and one that will apparently function effectively for a variety of leaders across a variety of leadership situations. But different leadership roles, across different functions, in different organisations and in different sectors will all require different leaders with different capabilities and different qualities. And after all, what makes great leaders great, at any level, are not their similarities, but their differences.

So, what are your differences? What are the differences that make you better at what you do rather than the person across the table from you? What are the differences that might make you better at leading your team over your predecessor or your potential successor? Can these differences be embraced or are you required to move them into the shadow, and if so, what impact does that have on your leadership?

Further Reading:

Fusco, T. et al (2013). *A Group-Coaching approach to Authentic Leadership Development.* Coaching Psychology International, 6, 2. 9-14. The International Society of Coaching Psychology. UK.

PATHOLOGICAL LEADERSHIP

P is for **Pathological Leadership**

"A political leader who creates conflicting agencies, who sets forth irreconcilable policies and who thinks he conquers when he divides is a person externalising profound splits and conflicts in his own psychological makeup." [59]

This chapter continues our sideways look at authentic leadership and, like the chapter on Hitler, it helps our understanding of authentic leadership indirectly by showing us what it isn't. Hitler's radical ideology was born from an obsessive and neurotic mind that became borderline and eventually psychotic and unhinged from reality. But what about leaders who don't suffer mental illness but do demonstrate a personality disorder. Technically, this is how you describe psychopathy. Psychopathic leadership entirely self-serves the leader and, unlike authentic leadership, has deleterious effects on the leader's followers and the teams and

---

[59] Waite, R. G. L. (1977). *Adolf Hitler: The Psychopathic God*. Basic Books: New York.

organisations under their charge. Where authentic leadership has a positive emotional and psychological impact on its followers, psychopathic leadership diminishes and damages them.

In bringing the idea of psychopathic leadership to life, we again consider a case study. Consider the quote above: *'a political leader who creates conflicting agencies, who sets forth irreconcilable policies and who thinks he conquers when he divides is a person externalising profound splits and conflicts in his own psychological makeup'* [60]. Which leader do you think this was written about? Where Hitler was perhaps an unsurprising subject for psychotic leadership, the subject for psychopathic leadership may (or may not) surprise you!

There are a few fascinating facts about psychopathy. First, is just how common it is, apparently around 1% of the general population. That means there are statistically 81,360 psychopaths walking the streets of London, nearly 11,000 in Birmingham, over 5,000 in Manchester and even 1,013 in my own small county town of Worcester. A second astonishing fact is just how prevalent and effective they are in business. There are four times more Psychopaths present in the

---

[60] Waite, R. G. L. (1977). *Adolf Hitler: The Psychopathic God.* Basic Books: New York.

business population than in the general population, meaning that there are 1.3m psychopaths in total currently working in the UK, including 280 at Google in London, 200 at Facebook and 160 at The Bank of England. Perhaps the most interesting thing about psychopaths though, is just how high functioning they can appear. Despite Hollywood's tendency to depict them as deranged murderers, the vast majority of psychopaths live relatively normal lives within society. They are cold and manipulative, but more often than not, far removed from their typical Hitchcock personas. Though many psychopaths are in prison because of violent crime, many more are incarcerated because of white-collar crime such as fraud, inside-trading and embezzlement. So, what exactly are psychopaths?

Technically psychopaths don't suffer from a mental illness, but a personality disorder characterised by lying, manipulation, deceit, egocentricity and other destructive anti-social behaviours. These are usually measured by Robert Hare's Psychopathy Checklist – the PCL. This checklist is based on items relating to emotional, interpersonal, behavioural and lifestyle traits. For over twenty years, statistical studies on criminal populations, psychiatric populations and the general population have shown the PCL to be highly effective in measuring psychopathy. Many people may score high on several of the items on the checklist, but true psychopaths score high on all of the items which include:

- Superficial charm
- Grandiose sense of self-worth
- Need for stimulation
- Pathological lying
- Manipulative
- Lack of remorse or guilt
- Shallow emotions
- Callous and lack of empathy
- Parasitic lifestyle
- Poor behavioural control
- Impulsive
- Irresponsible
- Deceitful
- Criminal versatility

Psychopaths can at first appear intelligent, impressive and charismatic. On the surface they don't seem to suffer from the irrational or delusional thinking that can characterise a mental disorder. However, psychopaths are consummate liars without conscience or loyalty to anyone but themselves. They live predatory lives where others don't tend to exist in their minds except as targets, objects or obstacles to be manoeuvred and exploited. Psychopaths operate without guilt or empathy and are incapable of feeling normal emotions other than more primitive ones such as anger, frustration and rage. This emotional barrenness has been the subject of neurological research using brain-imaging technology. Results from such MRI research shows that when presented with unpleasant stimuli (such as gruesome crime-scene photos) the area of the psychopath's brain that shows activity is not the normal area associated with emotional processing, but the area involved with language production and comprehension. Material that most people would find frightening or repulsive the psychopath finds intellectually interesting. They cognitively appraise the material without the visceral emotional reactions most normal people would experience. Needless to say, such cold, manipulative egocentricity means there is a preponderance of psychopaths to be found in business and political leadership. There are the malignant psychopathic despots to be found in developing countries or failed nations but there are also the seemingly odd-but-otherwise-normal psychopathic leaders in the developed world. For example, is Donald Trump one? Although not qualified to technically answer this question, I nonetheless invite you to join me in an investigative game of – is there a psychopath in The White House?

In 2016, 33 psychiatrists and psychologists from US mental health organisations signed an open letter to *The New York Times* (and later published in a book [61]) warning how unsuitable they considered Donald Trump for the presidency. In so doing they broke their own self-imposed silence around the evaluation of public figures. They believed that at such a critical time and with so much at stake, they owed their expertise to Congress and to the nation. What did they have to say? They said that Trump's speech and actions demonstrated an inability to tolerate views different from his own which would lead to rage reactions. His words and behaviour suggested a profound inability to empathise. And that individuals with these traits tended to distort reality to suit their own psychological state, attacking facts they didn't like and those who conveyed them. They went on to say that such attacks were likely to increase as the personal myth of his greatness would appear to be confirmed by his appointment as president. They

---

[61] Lee, B. X. (Eds). (2017). *The Dangerous Case of Donald Trump*. Thomas Dunn Books. NY.

concluded that the grave emotional instability of his speech and actions made Trump incapable of serving safely as president. Yet the country still voted him into The White House.

In *Fire and Fury* [62] Michael Wolff tells us that Trump's friends, advisors and business associates were all dumbfounded when he won the US election,

"Shortly after eight o'clock that evening, when the unexpected trend – that Trump might actually win – seemed confirmed… he looked like he had seen a ghost. There was, in the space of an hour, in Steve Bannon's observation, a befuddled Trump morphing into a disbelieving Trump and then into a quite horrified Trump. But still to come was the final transformation: suddenly Donald Trump became a man who believed that he deserved to be and was wholly capable of being the president of the United States" (p.18).

And so, the show began. Trump did not enjoy his inauguration. Many A-list stars had snubbed the event declining his invites, making Trump angry and hurt. The traditional evening event at the Lincoln Memorial was absent any star attraction so Trump took to the stage as the featured act angrily insisting that he could

---

[62] Wolff, M. (2017). *Fire and Fury*. Little Brown. London.

outdraw any star. In the hours before the event, Washington held its collective breath. *"An inauguration is supposed to be a love-in. The media gets a new upbeat story. For the party faithful, happy times are here again. For the country, it's a coronation"* [63] (p.42). But Trump felt shunned on the very day he became president and believed Washington failed to properly greet and celebrate him. The next day Trump sought confirmation that the inauguration had been a huge success, *"That crowd went all the way back. There were more than a million people at least, right?"* (p.42). Allegedly, among Trump's first moves as president was to have a series of inspirational photographs in the West Wing replaced with images of big crowd scenes at his inauguration. *"Hence, within twenty-four hours of the inauguration, the president had invented a million or so people who did not exist. He sent his new press secretary, Sean Spicer to argue his case… (and) blamed Spicer for not making the million phantom souls seem real"* (p.47). In an added surreal moment, the next day, Kellyanne Conway asserted the new president's right to claim 'alternative facts' and basically recast reality. So began Trump's incessant lying, literally from day one (and as of April 2020, these have been calculated by *The Washington Post* to total 18,000 - on average 15 lies for every

---

[63] Wolff, M. (2017). *Fire and Fury*. Little Brown. London.

single day of his presidency!). But this also forced the staff to become complicit in those lies, most publicly his Press Secretaries Sean Spicer and then Sarah Huckabee Saunders who had to defend and repeat his lies. So, began the reign of a president who appeared unable to control his compulsive need to exaggerate, mislead and lie. But it was not just his interminable lying that was of concern.

Most close to Trump agree that he is wholly lacking the one main requirement for the job, what neuroscientists call *executive function*. He apparently has no ability to plan, organise, pay attention, switch focus or understand wider cause-and-effect, making for a wholly unsettled White House. His advisors say that the president's views on foreign policy are random and uninformed. He is impressed by a general's military command experience, such as John Kelly and James Mattis, and wants them to lead on foreign policy, but then doesn't want to listen to them or take their advice. He has zero experience in foreign policy yet has no respect either for the experts who do. It was during his early intelligence briefings that alarm bells started ringing among his campaign staff. *"He seemed to lack the ability to take in third-party information and… seemed almost phobic about having formal demands on his attention. He stone-walled every written page and balked at every explanation"* [64] (p.115). By all accounts Trump simply doesn't do formal information. He doesn't do data or detail. A huge potential problem when it comes to evaluating political, diplomatic and military issues. *"Virtually innumerate, he was bored by both numbers and logistics – or worse, they gave him something like brain freeze. He absorbed nothing"* [65] (p.113). A senior White House official recalled an important military meeting held six months into Trump's presidency that had left all present baffled and concerned at his inability to think of world security and trade in a globally-connected manner, *"It seems clear that many of the president's senior advisors, especially those in the national security realm, are extremely concerned with his erratic nature, his relative ignorance, his inability to learn, as well as what they consider his dangerous views"* [66] (p.226). The meeting was part history lesson and part geostrategy – it was never going to hold the president's attention. It was a masterclass on the global democratic order and how it brought security, stability and prosperity. It included vast maps showing all the US interests overseas

---

[64] Wolff, M. (2017). *Fire and Fury*. Little Brown. London.

[65] Wolff, M. (2019). *Siege*. Little Brown. London.

[66] Woodward, B. (2018). *Fear: Trump in The White House*. Simon & Schuster. New York.

including; military sites, nuclear weapon sites, diplomatic postings, intelligence assets, treaties and trade deals. *"This is what has kept the peace for 70 years"* [67] (p.220) Tillerson said. Trump then went on to lecture and insult the entire group about how they didn't know anything about defence or national security. Witnessing Trump's complete inability to comprehend the connected intricacies presented to him, nor his willingness to try to learn, after the briefing, Rex Tillerson leant back in his chair and summed up the general mood in the room, *"He's a fucking moron"* [68] (p.225).

Trump's chief strategist, Steve Bannon, described him as having a simple on-off switch. On, he is full of false flattery, off, he is bitter, angry and resentful. As president-elect he wore his bitter grievances on his sleeve and then even as president, he continued to display unfiltered and uncontrollable displays of resentment and ire. Such a lack of basic impulse control accounts for his characteristic hyperbole and exaggeration. *"If he wanted something, his focus might be sharp, attentive and lavish, but if someone wanted something*

---

[67] Woodward, B. (2018). *Fear: Trump in The White House.* Simon & Schuster. New York.

[68] Woodward, B. (2018). *Fear: Trump in The White House.* Simon & Schuster. New York.

from him, he tended to become irritable and quickly lost interest. He demanded you pay him attention, then decided you were weak for grovelling" [69] (p.71). In sum, he is described as an energetic child and someone with little calculation and an attention that only exists in the moment, influenced simply by the last person he speaks to. As a consequence, the Trump White House has no real structure or order but is based on one man at the top and everyone else scrambling for his attention – just as it was in Trump Tower.

In summary then, Trump doesn't process information in the usual sense, has zero capacity for detail and, by all accounts, doesn't even read! *"Some believed that for all practical purposes he was no more than semiliterate… or postliterate – total television"* (p.114). *"But not only didn't he read, he didn't listen. He preferred to be the one talking. And he trusted his own expertise – no matter how paltry or irrelevant"* (p.114). A key tactic for managing such a president is apparently to just stall and kick the can further down the road until something else grabs his attention. Whatever the issue, he is apparently soon onto something else. Is it not strange that the job of US President does not entail any form of IQ assessment? In all conscience, would you hire

---

[69] Wolff, M. (2017). *Fire and Fury*. Little Brown. London.

someone for even a lower-level leadership position in your own organisation if in their selection interview they confessed to never reading anything, had a poor attention span, didn't like detail and weren't interested in logistics or strategy? And that despite and a chronic lack of relevant experience, believed they knew it all anyway?

Trump's approach to debate and decisions is also akin to that of a school child. Concrete, black and white and highly personalised and irresponsible, *"He hopelessly personalised everything"* [70] (p.215) Bannon would say. *"The notion of the presidency as an institutional and political concept ... was quite beyond him"* (p.219). Take his decision to sack FBI Director James Comey who headed up the investigation into alleged Russian involvement in the US elections and whose focus was turning increasingly to the Oval Office and the president himself. In Trump's mind, as always, this was not a problem to address but an opponent to focus on and attack. His approach to argument doesn't involve debate, disputation, refutation, counter argument, contradiction or critique – it focuses solely on ad hominem. That is, personal attacks on both the psychological and physical

---

[70] Wolff, M. (2017). *Fire and Fury*. Little Brown. London.

character of his opponents. This combined with his infamous name-calling really exemplifies an approach to argument that most people leave behind in the schoolyard. He defends himself by ridiculing others. The most famous examples were of course 'Crooked' Hilary Clinton and 'Little Rocket Man' Kim Jong Un. But those on his own side were not immune. Chief of Staff Kelly was a 'twitcher', Rex Harrison his Secretary of State was 'Rex the family dog', Reince Preibus, another Chief of Staff, was 'a weak midget and a little rat who scurries around', Chief Strategist Bannon was 'and looked like shit', his son-in-law Kushner was 'a suck-up', Kellyanne Conway was 'a cry-baby', Comey 'a stiff', Sessions was 'Mr Magoo'. Then there is Elizabeth 'Pocahontas' Warren, 'crying' Chuck Schumer and of course 'sleepy' Joe Biden. *"Insult trauma radiated out of the Oval Office you could hear it when passing by"* [71] (p.242).

After *The Washington Post* published details of the Access Hollywood tape that caught Trump boasting about sexually assaulting women, all of his campaign team cancelled their Sunday morning TV appearances scheduled for the next day. All but Rudy Giuliani, who appeared on all five Sunday talk shows to defend

---

[71] Wolff, M. (2017). *Fire and Fury*. Little Brown. London.

Trump. He agreed that the alleged behaviour was awful and reprehensible but said the presidential campaign experience would make Trump a changed man. Trump's response when they met later that evening was, *"Rudy, you're a baby! I've never seen a worse defence of me in my life. They took your diaper off right there. You're like a little baby that needed to be changed. When are you going to be a man? You're weak Rudy."* [72] (p.37). He is also reported to have given the following advice to an associate who had acknowledged similar lewd behaviour towards women, *"You've got to deny, deny, deny and push back on these women. If you admit to anything and any culpability, then you're dead. You've got to deny anything that's said about you. Never admit"* (p.175).

Many White House staff tried to control Trump's impulsive outbursts on Twitter, but to no avail. He says it's his megaphone and his way to communicate to the world without any filter and to cut through the noise and fake news *"That's the only way I have to communicate. I have tens of millions of followers. This is bigger than cable news"* [73] (p.205). After one particularly insulting tweet his chief of staff went to see him about

---

[72] Woodward, B. (2018). *Fear: Trump in The White House*. Simon & Schuster. New York.

[73] Woodward, B. (2018). *Fear: Trump in The White House*. Simon & Schuster. New York.

it and he just responded, *"I know what you are going to say, it's not presidential. And guess what, I know it. But I had to do it anyway"* (p.205). Even after he was warned that his ill-considered and irresponsible tweeting could get him into a war with Kim Jong Un he just said, *"This is who I am. This is how I communicate."* (p.206). For someone not considered thoughtful or erudite, his response to Twitter increasing their character use is rather amusing. He thought he could use the extra characters to flesh out his thoughts and add more 'depth' but still added, *"it's a bit of a shame because I was the Ernest Hemmingway of 140 characters"* (p.207).

Another character of psychopaths is their lack of emotion. They are devoid of social emotions such as love, joy, guilt, remorse, shame, pity or compassion but wholly capable of the more primitive and destructive emotions of anger and rage, emotions that White House staff have to endure on an almost daily basis. After he fired Comey, the FBI Chief revealed to *The New York Times* that Trump had basically asked him to drop his investigation into his National Security Advisor Michael Flynn. When it became clear that Comey had turned the tables on him, and commentators were starting to suggest it could lead him into impeachment territory, Trump became furious. Then when it was announced the next day that Robert Mueller had also been appointed to look into any Russian connection with the Trump election campaign *"The president erupted into uncontrollable anger... it was a harrowing experience"* [74] (p.165). He was glued to cable news for hour after hour raging at the television coverage *"Everybody's trying to get me. It's unfair. Now everybody's saying I'm going to be impeached"* (p.165). He believed the whole system was rigged against him, the institutions, the intelligence agencies, the lying media – a reliable topic of conversation with him was always his self-pitying and paranoid ramblings about *the possible martyrdom of Donald Trump* [75] (p.158).

It is generally accepted that (psychopathy aside) Trump also suffers from the Narcissistic Personality Disorder that we met under 'H' seeing everything in terms of its impact on him. (By way of a reminder, Narcissistic Personality Disorder is defined by; a lack of empathy, a grandiose sense of self-importance and entitlement, a preoccupation with fantasies of unlimited success, and a requirement for excessive admiration. When this includes antisocial and destructive behaviour it is termed *malignant narcissism* which is difficult to distinguish from psychopathy).

---

[74] Woodward, B. (2018). *Fear: Trump in The White House*. Simon & Schuster. New York.

[75] Wolff, M. (2017). *Fire and Fury*. Little Brown. London.

"They're out to get me. This is an injustice. This is unfair. How could this have happened?" (p.166) Trump raged for hours, reminding some onlookers of Nixon's final days in office as both their behaviours veered into paranoid territory. Politico even ran a piece on Trump's anger issues saying that *"... anger serves as a way to manage staff, express his displeasure or simply as an outlet that soothes him"* (p.253). Alarmed staff tend to deal with his anger and volatility by either leaving him alone or simply agreeing with him whatever he says.

Trump is also said to encourage aggressive disagreement throughout the West Wing (though not with him) and appears to enjoy the chaos and churn it creates beneath him. Such leadership tends to create a Darwinian environment where everyone is out for themselves – a breeding ground for anxiety and paranoia. In his second book on the Trump presidency *Siege* [76] Michael Wolff described the first few months as not so much a political drama as a psychodrama *"Here was a volatile and uncertain president, releasing, almost on a daily basis, his strange furies on the world and, at the same time, on his own staff"* (p.x). Trump's first Chief of Staff described the atmosphere of distrust he created as *"... thick and corrosive. The*

---

[76] Wolff, M. (2019). *Siege*. Little Brown. London.

atmosphere was primitive; everyone was ostensibly on the same side, but they had seemed suited up in battle armour, particularly the president" [77] (p.225). When Reince Priebus, another Chief of Staff, left The White House he concluded that Trump surrounds himself with *"...high-ranking natural killers with no requirement to produce regular work products – a plan, a speech, a strategy, a budget, a work schedule. They were... a band of chaos creators"* (p.236). Trump had flatly failed the Lincoln test to put a team of his own rivals and critics at the top table. He had actually gone one further and surrounded himself with *"... the dysfunctional and inept., because he was dysfunctional and inept. Only in the land of the blind could he be king"* [78] (p.202). Even worse, Priebus said, *"He puts natural predators at the table. Not just rivals – predators. If you have natural predators at the table, things don't move."* (p.237). And so, things didn't progress anywhere; health, tax, foreign policy, nothing. Any attempts at progress were described as incomplete, inconsistent and incoherent.

So why do the professionals stay? Some think because of a higher obligation or rationale, believing *"The White House needed normal, sane, logical, adult professionals.*

---

[77] Woodward, B. (2018). *Fear: Trump in The White House*. Simon & Schuster. New York.

[78] Wolff, M. (2017). *Fire and Fury*. Little Brown. London.

To a person, these pros saw themselves bringing positive attributes – rational minds, analytical powers, significant professional experience – to a situation sorely lacking those things" [79] (p.185). Maybe they remain to try and stop the worst from happening and to try and make the unstable and abnormal, as stable and normal as possible. Many consider themselves the possible antidote to Trump and his "… *chaos, impulsiveness and stupidity*" (p.185). But all this comes at a cost.

A quick search of www.Google.Scholar research papers show ample evidence for the psychological benefits of authentic leadership to followers. Authentic leadership empowers and enhances whereas pathological leadership tends to diminish and damage. In *Down the Rabbit Hole of Leadership* [80] Professor of Leadership Manfred Kets de Vries gives us a closer insight into just how this happens. As both a management scholar and a psychoanalyst Kets de Vries applies clinical psychology to his studies of management and leadership and seems in no doubt about the question we are exploring, stating that Trump is a:

---

[79] Wolff, M. (2017). *Fire and Fury*. Little Brown. London.

[80] Kets de Vries, M. (2019). *Down the Rabbit Hole of Leadership: Leadership Pathology in Everyday Life*. Palgrave Macmillan. Switzerland.

"... larger-than-life lesson in personality theory, an unholy alliance of a narcissistic personality disorder blended with psychopathic behaviour. Typically, people suffering from a narcissistic personality disorder have a grandiose sense of self-importance. Their world centres on power, success and appearances. They exaggerate their achievements and talents and are cocky, self-centred, and manipulative. In addition, they feel a strong sense of entitlement, always expecting special treatment. Furthermore, many narcissists lack empathy. And behind this mask of super-confidence, we often find a person with a fragile self-esteem, vulnerable to the slightest criticism. In terms of psychopathy, many of these people may appear normal, even charming, but also display persistent antisocial behaviour. Their lack of conscience and empathy, and their inability to feel attached to people, contributes to a predatory lifestyle. Trump fits this unholy dyad to a T" (p.26).

Kets de Vries compares the Trump White House to a medieval court whose courtiers have decided that the only way to survive his reign is through submission and subservience - which comes at a high cost to their own personal dignity and authenticity. He believes Trump is a *"... wounded and quite disturbed individual"* [81] (p.26) who personally denigrates all who disagree with him with spite, envy and vindictiveness. A basic

---

[81] Kets de Vries, M. (2019). *Down the Rabbit Hole of Leadership: Leadership Pathology in Everyday Life.* Palgrave Macmillan. Switzerland.

operating principle of the Trump White House is that you simply don't talk back to him or disagree with him. If you do you immediately become an enemy or a *nonperson*. So evident is his inability to take criticism or engage in any form of debate about policy issues that most staff very quickly give up trying. In summary, Kets de Vries says,

"... this kind of acting out would raise fewer flags if he were running for office in a banana republic. We are talking however, about the highest office in the most important country in the world. His presidency has implications not only for the United States, but also for the rest of the planet. Is he the kind of person we want to have with a finger on the nuclear button?" (p.26).

Or as Hilary Clinton put it, *"A man you can bait with a tweet is not a man we can trust with nuclear weapons"* [82] (p.301). The list of what makes this man uniquely unqualified to be president of the US is legion; incompetence, impulsiveness, lack of responsibility, lack of knowledge, lack of experience, attention deficit, inability to listen, unwillingness to learn, racist, misogynist, a vain, aggressive lying bully prone to outburst of vengeful and sadistic rage. Which is not, I'm hopeful the reader will agree, a consummate

---

[82] Woodward, B. (2018). *Fear: Trump in The White House.* Simon & Schuster. New York.

demonstration of authentic leadership. It is more a strident case of pathological leadership that Kets de Vries summaries when he states simply *"No other American President in modern history has demonstrated this degree of character pathology"* [83] (p.26).

As I finish this chapter, we are now starting to see some high-ranking officials break with tradition and comment on their former boss who is still sitting in the Oval Office. The likes of Generals John Kelly and James Mattis. General Mattis is decrying the complete absence of mature leadership in the last three years and General Kelly is suggesting that all future presidential candidates be *put through the filter* and assessed for their ethics and their temperament. The world can only hope, and in the meantime they have on record details of at least thirty-three psychiatrists and psychologists who would certainly be happy to help with that task!

Further Reading:

Frank, J. A. (2018). *Trump on the Couch: Inside the Mind of the President.* Avery: Penguin, Random

---

[83] Kets de Vries, M. (2019). *Down the Rabbit Hole of Leadership: Leadership Pathology in Everyday Life.* Palgrave Macmillan. Switzerland.

Hare, R. D. (1995). *Without Conscience: The Disturbing World of the Psychopaths Among Us.* The Guildford Press. New York.

Hare, R. D. (2007). *Snakes in Suits: When Psychopaths go to Work.* HarperCollins: New York.

Johnston, D. C. (2018). *It's Even Worse Than You Think: What the Trump Administration is Doing to America.* Simon & Schuster. New York.

Ronson, J. (2011). *The Psychopath Test: A Journey Through the Madness Industry.* Picador: London.

Sperry, L. (2003). *Handbook of Diagnosis and Treatment of DSM-IV-TR Personality Disorders.* (2nd Ed). Brunner-Routledge: New York.

Qualitative vs Quantitative

Q is for **Qualitative** & **Quantitative** Assessment

In a recent survey of 96 Fortune 500 CEOs, 92 said they were interested in learning the business impact of their leadership development programmes, but only 4 of them said that was currently happening in their own business. ROI Institute [84] research also shows that only 10 per cent of development programmes generally are being evaluated at the return on investment level and almost 90 per cent at just the immediate reaction level. This chapter will explore the implications of what this means for Authentic Leadership Development (ALD).

Typically, leadership programme evaluations are (or

---

[84] Philips, P. P., Philips, J. P., Stone. R. D., & Burkett, H. Butterworth Heinemann. (2007). *The ROI Field Book: Strategies for Implementing ROI in HR and Training.* Elsevier. Oxford. UK.

could be) capturing evaluation data at five different levels.

Level 1 evaluation is about reaction-level data. This simply gauges participants' immediate reaction to the content and format of a programme. Depending on the questions asked this may be interesting for an immediate assessment of a programme's 'face validity' in terms of content and delivery but is of questionable value in estimating the impact the programme will have after the leaders return to work.

Level 2 evaluation is about learning. This is the new knowledge individuals gain from participating in a development programme. This can be assessed to some degree immediately upon course completion, but again, this is a highly unreliable prediction of what learning will be retained and used by an individual afterwards. Most learning and development (L&D) evaluation stops at this level with the typical course evaluation 'happy sheet' given out directly at the end of the programme, which is of course far too early to say what learning will be applied. Such application questions can only really be asked after the programme is complete and participants have returned to their workplace. This is the focus of the next level of evaluation.

Level 3 evaluation is about application/implementation – this is the extent to which individuals have actually adjusted and changed their behaviours and implemented what they have learnt. Evaluation at this level is critical to understanding what learning from a programme actually makes its way back to the workplace and is implemented by the leader. Astonishingly, this accounts for just over a third of evaluations - at 34 per cent!

Higher levels of evaluations are even more rare as they attempt to identify the impact of learning and behaviour change on business measures and in turn translate this into a concrete monetary value or Return on Investment (ROI).

Level 4 is impact – this is the consequence of changes that have been implemented and represent the positive and tangible impact within the leader's own environment, such as increased productivity, quality, cost saving etc. To evidence a true relationship between the programme and its impact, a direct link has to be established connecting the two (as discussed under 'O'). This can be notoriously difficult, so it is suggested programme design be aligned with specific business measures prior to delivery if there is to be any hope of successfully isolating the effects of the programme from other influences impacting the same business measure. This can be quite a demanding and complex task and is probably the reason why a majority of L&D evaluation stops short of this level. According to ROI Institute figures, this is something two-thirds of organisations simply never pursue. In evaluation terms this is quite unsatisfactory and apparently wouldn't best please 92 out of 96 top 500 CEO's!

Even if there is an excuse for a lack of Level 4 evaluation due to time, logistics or cost, there really isn't one for two thirds of organisations not even bothering with a Level 3 follow-up to see what behaviour change has actually been achieved, implemented and maintained. This is vital data, because if you're still doing something differently after three months and it has survived the typical post-programme atrophy, then the chances are very high that it represents a permanent shift in approach or performance.

Evaluation Level 5 is return on investment (R.O.I). This level of evaluation compares the monetary value of the impact with the overall cost of the programme. This is common accounting practice that can establish the cost/benefit ratio of things like capital equipment, property, etc., but is fraught with complications when trying to assess the same for learning and development, where the exact lines of cause and effect within complex organisational systems are difficult to isolate and correlate. So, where does all this leave us in terms of Authentic Leadership Development?

Even the ROI Institute acknowledges that not all programmes should progress to the ROI level of evaluation but can still be evaluated by capturing their intangible benefits. Most of the benefits of increased personal and professional authenticity will most likely fall into this intangible category. This is not to say these are of any less importance than the tangible benefits, just that they represent benefits even the ROI Institute says cannot, indeed should not, be converted into a monetary value, despite them still providing very important evaluation data. The Institute describes intangible assets as *"The key to competitive advantage. But invisible, difficult to quantify, and not tracked through traditional accounting practices"* (p.196). One obvious example of an intangible benefit is employee satisfaction. This can be monitored and analysed as a good health check of an organisation without any further attempt needed to convert the data into a monetary value. Other intangible benefits may include:

- Staff and stakeholder engagement
- Positive organisational citizenship
- Team empowerment and motivation
- Positive workforce and company culture

Most benefits of ALD are of the intangible type, relating to such attributes as self-awareness, self-regulation and self-confidence. Many participants of this form of development report a new ability to elevate their gaze up from their immediate day-to-day operational issues and out towards the horizon, where they can see and appreciate the more long-term, complex and systemic issues that they should be focusing on in their leadership. Others more proactively lean into their next level of responsibility while feeling more (re)energised and take on greater responsibilities while feeling more resourceful and resilient as they do so. While perhaps less immediately tangible, all of these things are striking examples of shifts in performance and perspective [85] that underscore the transformative power of genuine authentic leadership development.

---

[85] Fusco, T. (2018). *An Evidence-based Approach to Authentic Leadership Development*. Routledge: Oxford.

More of the outcomes of ALD group-coaching will be covered under 'W' and 'X'.

R is for **Rogers**

"It seems to me that at bottom each person is asking, who am I really? How can I get in touch with this real self... how can I become myself?" [86] Carl Rogers

Each area of study has its classic texts and in the field of psychology Carl Rogers *On Becoming a Person* [87] is one such classic. The book derives its title from its central thesis that it is each person's ultimate conscious and unconscious goal to become fully *themselves*. Carl Rogers was what is known as a Humanistic Psychotherapist. He did not subscribe to any existing psychotherapeutic orthodoxy such as Freuds' Psychoanalysis or Jung's Psychoanalytic Psychology, nor did he use the tools or techniques of Cognitive or

---

[86] Rogers, C. (1961). *On Becoming a Person.* Constable & Co. London.
[87] Rogers, C. (1961). *On Becoming a Person.* Constable & Co. London.

Behavioural therapy. His philosophy and technique were based on establishing genuine and meaningful contact and dialogue with each and every individual he worked with. He also believed in the curious paradox of human change, that only when you fully accept yourself as you are, can you change. His conditions of therapy created the kind of environment that allowed and enabled his clients to fully understand and accept who they are. And then, only then, personal change could and invariably did occur.

In this classic book Rogers talks about a lecture invitation he received one year to deliver a talk entitled *'This is Me'*, which was a lecture series that invited speakers to talk about themselves as much as about their work. Below is a part summary of this lecture that gives us a fascinating insight into personal authenticity as offered by one of the world's most gifted psychotherapists.

Lesson 1: *"I find I am more effective when I can listen acceptingly to myself"* (p.17).

Rogers believed that becoming better at listening to himself helped him know what he was feeling at any given moment which in turn helped him become more adequate in letting himself be what he was, "*It becomes easier for me to accept myself as a decidedly imperfect person*" (p.17). He acknowledged that this imperfect self-acceptance might sound strange to some but he believed its value lay in the curious paradox his own experience had taught him, that you need to accept yourself to change yourself "… *We cannot move away from what we are, until we thoroughly accept what we are… then change seems to come about almost unnoticed*" (p.17).

Lesson 2: "*In my relationships with persons I have found that it does not help, in the long run, to act as though I were something that I am not*" (p.16).

Rogers is saying that he had never found it helpful or effective in building constructive relations with others, to present a façade. He believed it was quite unhelpful to act one way on the surface when feeling something quite different inside. And that most of the mistakes he made in interpersonal encounters were as a result of him behaving one way on the surface while having completely contrary feelings underneath.

Lesson 3: "*I have found it of enormous value when I can permit myself to understand and accept another person*" (p.18).

A key reason why this is so difficult he says is that when listening to another's views and beliefs, our first instinct is one of evaluation not understanding. We effortlessly appraise others, e.g. that's right or wrong, rational or irrational, wise or ignorant. The reason for this is that when we genuinely permit ourselves to fully understand another, we risk being changed ourselves by that understanding. Talking of his encounters with clients Rogers would say that each encounter both enriched and changed him. But even more important is that the genuine listening to and understanding of another, permits *them* to change. It helps them to access, understand and accept the myriad of feelings and beliefs, positive and negative, that make up their individual experience. Rogers was convinced from personal experience and professional observation, that the more one is willing and able to be themselves the more naturally change will occur, he called this - "*A very paradoxical thing*" (p.22).

Lesson 4: "*I can trust my experience*" (p.22).

Rogers says that it took him a very long time to finally learn that when something *feels* like it is worth doing then it *is* worth doing. He says he finally came to learn that his overall embodied sense of a situation was more trustworthy than just his intellectual evaluation of it. He says he had never regretted taking a decision that *felt* right even if he had harboured some intellectual doubts about it at the time. He says when he trusted his inner-sense, he invariably discovered some wisdom in what might have initially appeared an unconventional move *"As I gradually come to trust my own reactions more deeply, I find that I can use them to guide my thinking. I have come to have more respect for those vague thoughts which occur in me from time to time, which feel as though they are significant. I am inclined to think that these unclear thoughts or hunches will lead me to important areas. I think of it as trusting the totality of my experience, which I learned to suspect is wiser than my intellect. It is fallible I am sure, but I believe it to be less fallible than my conscious mind alone"* (p.23).

Lesson 5: *"The evaluation of others is not a guide for me"* (p.23).

Rogers believed that while the opinions and judgements of others should be listened to and accepted for what they are, they could never be an objective guide for himself. He firmly believed that in the final analysis only one person could really know whether what he was doing was honest, open and sound - or not. And of course, he alone was that person. He was always willing to receive positive and negative feedback and criticism and praise, but he knew the task of weighing this feedback, its meaning and its usefulness, was a task he could not relinquish to another.

Lesson 6: *"Persons have a basically positive direction"* (p.26).

Rogers also speaks of how we can help others become more authentically themselves. He believed that individuals have within them both the capacity and tendency towards growth and that this tendency actualises within a suitable psychological climate. He described this tendency as an urge which is evident in all organic life – to expand, extend, develop, mature, activate and express all the capacities of itself. Even in spite of the fact that this tendency can become deeply buried under layers of what he called *encrusted psychological defences hidden behind elaborate facades*. He believed this tendency simply awaits the proper psychological and relational conditions under which it can be released and expressed. Then the self gradually becomes more authentically self-aware, self-determining and self-congruent. When the requisite conditions of genuine and unconditional understanding and acceptance are created and when one individual feels truly received by another within such a safe psychological climate, they naturally begin to move away from their masks and facades. These conditions famously became known as *Rogerian conditions* and when present in a relationship, these qualities of warmth, empathy and genuine positive regard, have been evidenced to achieve profound personal growth, enabling individuals to:

- *see themselves differently*
- *accept themselves more fully*
- *become more self-confident and self-directing*
- *become more the person they would like to be*
- *adopt more realistic goals for themselves*
- *behave in a more mature fashion*
- *change their maladapted behaviours*
- *become more acceptant of others*

So, the questions you may consider from arguably the greatest humanist psychotherapist of them all, are quite simple, yet personally and professionally profound:

- What might happen if you listened more genuinely and acceptingly to yourself?
- What might happen in your relationships with others if, you were able to act more genuinely as yourself? What stops you now?
- What would happen if you decided to listen less to the evaluation of others and more to your own self-evaluation?
- What might you find of value if you were able to permit yourself to listen to, understand and accept others more as they are?
- How might your leadership be different if you were to believe that, all else being equal, the people you lead have a fundamental instinct for growth and self-determination?
- As an experiment, on a chosen occasion, press pause on your intellect and tune into your 'whole and embodied' experience of the situation – and see if it offers you any deeper sense of your situation?

All such paths of enquiry may potentially help you towards a more authentic way of being and leading.

Further Reading:

Fusco, T. et al (2014). *A Humanistic Approach to Authentic Leadership Development*. Coaching Psychology International, 7, 1. 11-16. The International Society of Coaching Psychology.

Kirschenbaum, H. (2007). *The Life and Works of Carl Rogers*. PCCS Books. Ross-on-Wye. UK.

Rogers, C. (1995). *A Way of Being*. Mariner Books. US.

Strategic Leadership

S is for Strategic Leadership

"I would like to die thinking that humanity has a bright future, to solve sustainable energy and be well on our way to becoming a multiplanetary species with a self-sustaining civilisation on another planet and so be able to cope with the worst-case scenario of extinguishing human consciousness."[88] Elon Musk

Man-on-Mars missions can strike some people as bizarre, but it has given Elon Musk a unique rallying cry for all of his companies. Musk is the founder and CEO of SolarCity, Tesla and SpaceX and it is this far-reaching galactic goal that forms the unifying principle over everything he does. Strategic leaders look naturally to the distant horizons - and they don't come much more distant than this. Employees at all his companies are well aware of this and well aware they are trying to achieve the impossible every day. When Musk sets unrealistic goals, rants at employees,

---

[88] Vance, A. (2016). *Elon Musk: How the Billionaire CEO of SpaceX and Tesla is Shaping our Future.* Random House. London.

and works them to the bone, it's understood to be all part of the 'Mars agenda'. It seems what Musk has developed, that so many in Silicon Valley lack, is a meaningful world view. He's like a possessed genius on the grandest quest ever conceived. Where Mark Zuckerberg wants to help you share photos, and sell advertising space, Musk is marshalling his troops and technology to save the human race from self-imposed or accidental annihilation.

While the rest of the aerospace industry has been content to keep sending what looks like relics from the 1960s into space, Musk and SpaceX have made a point of doing just the opposite. Its reusable rockets and reusable spaceships look like true 21st century machines and this modernisation of equipment is not just for show. It reflects a constant push to advance technology and change the economics of the industry. Musk does not want to simply lower the cost of deploying satellites and resupplying the space station. He wants to lower the cost of launches to the point that it becomes economical and practical to fly many thousands of supply trips to Mars and start a colony – he wants to conquer the solar system!

People say it is his drive and vision that makes them both tolerate him and become loyal to him. He has the ability to work harder and endure more stress than the other bosses most of his execs have worked for. They say that what he went through when he nearly lost everything in 2008 would have broken anyone else, but he kept working and stayed focussed. This ability to focus in the midst of a crisis stands as one of his main advantages over other competitors and executives. Most people under that sort of pressure fray and their decisions go bad. Whereas Musk gets hyperrational and is still able to make very clear, long-term decisions. The harder it gets, the better he gets.

People who have spent significant time with Musk also attest to his abilities to absorb incredible quantities of information with near flawless recall. At SpaceX, when employees think he is challenging them to see if they know their physics, they soon realise he is just trying to learn, and he continues to quiz them until he knows most of what they know. This is said to be one of his most impressive and intimidating skills. He also sets extremely aggressive delivery targets for very difficult-to-make products. He will pick the most aggressive time schedule imaginable assuming everything goes right, and then accelerate it by assuming that everyone can work harder and faster. One senior executive, sums this up, saying *"I don't want to be the person who ever has to compete with Elon.*

THE A TO Z OF AUTHENTIC LEADERSHIP

You might as well leave the business and find something else to do. He will outmanoeuvre you, outthink you and out-execute you" (p.102).

The story is similar at Tesla where Musk spends the other 50% of his working week. Before Elon Musk, Silicon Valley had done little of note in the automotive industry. Musk had never run a car factory before and was considered arrogant and amateurish by Detroit. Yet, one year after the Model S went on sale, Tesla posted a profit and hit $562m in quarterly revenue and became as valuable as Mazda. He had built the automotive equivalent of the iPhone leaving car execs in Detroit, Japan and Germany pondering what had just happened. Musk's mind is always way beyond the present and what just happened was that he did indeed out-think them, out-manoeuvre them and out-execute them.

The same rules apply at both Tesla and SpaceX in that Musk frequently overwhelms engineers with requests. It's like a binary experience for him in that either you're trying to make something spectacular without compromise, or you're not. And if you're not he considers you a failure. As tough and unreasonable as this philosophy may seem, it works for Musk and his mission as it constantly pushes both himself and those around him to their limits. It is sometimes forgotten that people thought the idea of building a desirable electric car was the worst business opportunity going and the venture capitalists were nowhere to be seen. But what separated Tesla from the competition was the willingness of Musk to charge after his vision without compromise. If Tesla achieves its ultimate vision to deliver an affordable car with a 500 miles range, something the auto industry insisted for years was impossible, along with the construction of its planned worldwide network of free charging stations, Musk will have achieved an exceptional feat in capitalist history.

Musk's third and smallest company (valued at $7bn) is SolarCity, the largest builder and installer of solar panels in the US and on schedule to become one of their major Utility companies. Both SolarCity and Tesla work together developing battery and charging technology for both cars and panels and as a result Musk owns the world's two most successful clean-tech companies. But like most of his ventures they do not represent simple business opportunities, as demonstrated by Tesla's open-source patent policy. Each of his businesses is interconnected in both the short and long term and are key to his audacious vision and unified theory. That is, through electric cars and solar energy he can save the planet, but through SpaceX he can develop an escape route, just in case.

Strategic Leaders

Elon Musk epitomises the Strategic Leader. Strategic Leaders have great 'systems intelligence' and highly developed organisation and engineering skills in both the ability to conceive of remote ends and the ability to design the long-range plans to accomplish them. Strategic leaders seek knowhow and will continue relentlessly in their efforts to understand – just so they can. They have an interest in power over nature and the ability to understand and perhaps even shape the universe itself, think Albert Einstein and Stephen Hawkins. They want to understand and control everything that is important to them whether it is to design a product or build a theory. If it is significant to them, they must be able to master it and know how to control it should they need to. Above all, in whatever domain is important to them, they must be competent, the foundation of their self-esteem depends on it. This all helps the Strategic leader secure greater autonomy, in which is rooted their self-respect. Incompetence is abhorrent, and it is a special curse that no one is more ruthlessly self-critical or demanding of their own behaviour than themselves. However well they have done in the past, that performance is only a benchmark for determining future performance and success: to rise above is to succeed and to fall short is to fail. Therefore, they must achieve and achieve again and always at a higher level of accomplishment. Their hunger for greater achievement presses them constantly throughout their lives, yet paradoxically they live on the very edge of failure since they will not allow themselves any regression in their constantly escalating standards.

Strategic leaders are born problem-solvers and think in terms of possibilities and probabilities while ignoring traditional views and ideas, ever on the lookout for systemic problems and bent on solving them. They will experiment to try and find more elegant and powerful models of understanding and control. They cannot help but notice problems, whether in logic or understanding, in a simple riddle or in the matters of the universe, they will try to apply their knowledge towards a resolution of such problems. If they are not given a problem, Strategic leaders will set themselves one just to check and exercise their understanding and abilities. They are natural reasoners and equate such reason with intelligence. Intelligence being something they value highly, despising any form of stupidity, especially in themselves.

In choice of occupation they favour and operate at their best working with systems more than material, tools or personnel. Whatever the type of system (mechanical, social, organic) and whatever the level of sophistication, it is the complexity itself that intrigues the Strategic leader. Famous Strategic leaders include the more far-sighted US presidents such as Dwight Eisenhower, Abraham Lincoln, Thomas Jefferson and scientific leaders and pioneers such as Albert Einstein and Thomas Edison.

How about you? Are you in your element gazing out to distant horizons? Working out how all the different pieces of your field and organisation fit together? Testing yourself? Working out your fifth or sixth move ahead? And testing yourself again? If your 'leadership home' is a long-term and abstract one it will influence all around you – for better and for worse. So, be the authentic wizard-leader you are… just ensure you have a team around you who are doing the less cerebral but still necessary immediate, concrete and detailed work!

TACTICAL LEADERSHIP

T is for Tactical Leadership

"Truth be told, Red didn't belong in the office at all, even at the best of times. The only place he ever felt comfortable was outdoors, on a job, in the midst of turmoil and chaos and crisis, in the jungles of Sumatra, or the mountains of Columbia, or the west Texas plains, when his ass was on the line."[89]

Red Adair (1915-2004) was a world-renowned American oil-well firefighter. He gained fame in Europe for tackling the Alpha Piper oil-rig disaster in the North Sea in the 1980s.

At 19 Red Adair was the youngest and most inexperienced working on his section of the railroad. Yet he designed a levering device that enabled him to unload coal from railroad cars faster than the more experienced men twice his size. It was made out of scrap lumber and cost nothing. When he was faced

---

[89] Singerman, P. (1990). *Red Adair: An American Hero: The Authorised Biography.* Bloomsbury: London.

with the problems of fighting oil well fires in the North Sea, 45 years later, he designed the Tharos, a huge twin-hulled, self-propelled, semi-submersible work barge that could perform just about any task imaginable in servicing and repairing offshore oil rigs. Whether a cheap make-do lever or a $100 million barge, it was all the same to Red Adair. He simply saw all obstacles – men, weather, fires – as hurdles in a race he would win, either by jumping over them or knocking them down.

Eventually Red got off the railroads and into the oil fields he'd been dreaming of. On his first walk into the oil field his companion asked, *"What do you think?"*. They were ankle-deep in a snake-infested swamp, covered in mud, mosquitoes, and thorny brambles - *"This is great!"* said Red. The oil field was filled with tails of the strange things' men had done when they were next to a well that blew. The roar of a blowout has caused men to lose control of their bowels, tear their clothes off in sheer panic, run screaming down a mountainside, into a river or a bramble thicket. Wild wells have driven bears out of hibernation, driven fish from the river and driven men mad. Once, at an oil well blowout in Sumatra, the sonic intensity disorientated a tiger so much that it rushed from the jungle into the drilling camp and leapt into a man-made reservoir where it swam in circles all night. It is said that nobody knows how they will behave when a well blows out, no more than they know how they will behave during an earthquake or under artillery fire. For the noise of a blowing well is so violent it drives a man beyond all reason to the point of a purely reflexive response. One reaction, however, has remained reasonably constant throughout the history of the oil field. When a well comes loose, every man working on it, no matter how tough, no matter how strong, will always run as fast and as far as he can to safety. It came as quite a shock then, to the others on a well in Arkansas when a visiting Red Adair stayed right where he was, beside the wellhead, two feet from a stream of gas forceful enough to cut him to pieces should he stumble into it. Very quickly Red Adair became famous for his nerve and composure under the madness of the oil fires.

Later, when Red Adair became well known in the oil field, the confidence he inspired would cause men to stay with him at a blowing well or follow him up to one on fire. On one particular day when a well blew he stood there all by himself, *in a cloud of natural gas spiked with petroleum vapour by a drilling rig, shuddering and clanking its way toward self-destruction while enveloped in an ever-thickening cloud of distillate – just about as explosive an environment you can find on earth.* All the other rig hands continued sprinting in every direction through the woods and over the fields trying to put enough distance between themselves and the well to keep from being burned to a crisp when it blew. It felt, to Red Adair, as though the earth itself had ruptured right next to him and was spewing its innards into the air, but *his* instinct, when confronted for the first time in his life by this unimaginably powerful natural force, was *not* to run. Instead of fear, he was gripped by the need to find out what was going wrong. Instead of being filled with terror, he was filled with an overwhelming desire to fix whatever was screwing up the hard work he'd been doing for a week. There was no way he was going to turn his back on it before he could figure out why it was making all that noise and how to stop it. He looked around and was able to see, through the veil of gas, that a valve had worked loose. He sorted it!

Even away from the oil field the only way Red could let off steam was by involving himself in a situation that created tension. If he couldn't create tension, he wasn't happy. The adrenalin had to pump, which is why he got some release from fighting well fires by going to the stock car racetrack and driving, and when he couldn't do that, by getting down in the racing pits where it was wild and greasy and loud. After car racing came boat racing. To keep his adrenaline pumping, if he wasn't on a job, he'd run boat marathons of 250-500 miles, one-hour races, six-hour races, oval circuit races, river races, lake races, 100mph through the water was relaxation to him. Red Adair was the archetypal Tactical Leader.

The Tactical Leader

The Tactical leader can be characterised by their remarkable attentiveness to the immediate environment and work in a practical and tactical way to optimise their position in the here and now. Whether these are skirmishes and manoeuvres on the sports field or in the boardroom. Tactical leaders are always scanning for opportunities, always looking for the best angle of approach, able to come up with the particular action which at that moment gives them the greatest advantage and chance of success. Tactical leaders can notice the smallest detail in their immediate surroundings, the slightest change in both foreground and background, which allow them to grasp the moment and to fully exploit whatever resources are at hand and turn them to their advantage. With their ears to the ground and their finger on the pulse, they can always spot an opening or an opportunity.

Tactical leaders are most at home in a world that is concrete, visible and audible and made up of objects and events that can be made and manipulated. They have far less interest in things that are abstract or of little practical use – if it can't be seen, touched or used, who needs it? But if it can be used – then use it! In fact, the Tactical leaders can have what is called 'function lust' and often cannot resist *just doing it!* - sail the boat, climb the hill, swim the lake, they *must* pull the metaphorical trigger. The occasional dark side of this can be an energetic compulsion towards the more reckless. The Tactical leader sees themselves, and wish to be seen by others, as bold, impressive and competitive. In fact, their self-confidence, self-respect and self-esteem depends on their ability to act daringly, impressively and competitively. They will not be outdone or overtaken and always have one eye on the next plot or the next shot. Tactical leaders show little interest in or patience for mere abstractions and consider theories or generalities mostly a waste of time. They are not inclined towards high-speculation or deep-meaning. After all, inward searching and deep reflection are the enemy of impulse and action. The Tactical leaders' orientation towards the concrete is even present in the way they think and speak descriptively. They will endure talk of high principles and long-range goals as long as it leads to action otherwise it will be quickly abandoned. If they are not excited by something, they will look for something to be excited by. The Tactical leader detests routine and the status quo and so important is impulse and action to them their motto could be – *make something happen!*

Immediate vigilance and opportunism make the Tactical Leader highly effective negotiators and they can spot things that give them an edge where others can't. For this reason, they make excellent troubleshooters and have no peer in negotiating tense situations. Most business leadership doesn't require particular feats of physical bravery, but the analogy of the 'burning platform' is often used in organisations when the heat is on and the metaphorical fires need fighting. Whether its manoeuvring intense negotiations, addressing a management crisis or negotiating a challenging merger, the Tactical leader with their incomparable nerve and skill in the moment, along with their exquisite ability to master their immediate environments, for sure, make them the Red Adairs of the business and political world, they include within their ranks; Winston Churchill, Franklin Roosevelt, JFK and Rupert Murdoch.

How about you? Are you in your element on 'the front line'? Is that a natural place for you? Where you lose yourself and all sense of time? If there's no metaphorical burning platform do you set one alight just so you can call action-stations and swoop into action, keeping your head while those around you seem to be losing theirs? If this is your 'leadership home' it will influence all around you – for better and for worse. So, be the action-hero leader you are… just ensure you have a team around you who are doing the less dramatic but necessary strategic and back-office work!

UNCERTAINTY

U is for **Uncertainty**

"The future of our organisations depends on successfully identifying and developing all leaders to higher LDLs, to a place of greater authenticity, so that they can respond effectively to the increasingly complex demands of our time." [90]

During 2 weeks in 1962 the world faced a potential global catastrophe. Hostile Soviet ships with nuclear missiles aboard were headed towards Cuba and into the western hemisphere for the first time. John F Kennedy was the U.S. President at the time and was charged with effectively navigating what was considered to be a genuine human existential crisis. Some of JFK's Joint Chiefs of Staff said that both airstrikes and an invasion were clearly necessary.

---

[90] Eigel, K. M., & Kuhnert, K. W. (2005). *Authentic Development: Leadership Development Level and Executive Effectiveness.* In Gardener, W., Avolio, B. and Walumba, F. (Eds) Authentic Leadership Theory and Practise: Origins, Effects and Development. Monographs in Leadership and Management, 3, Elsevier, Oxford, 357-385.

Others, including his Secretary of Defence, cautioned against aggression and advised proactive diplomacy with the Soviet state. An additional problem, however, was that the Soviet foreign minister had already lied to the US administration denying the existence of the missiles, despite photographic evidence to the contrary. So, what was JFK to do? Well, in the end he chose a firm response but one that stopped short of a direct attack on Cuba, establishing a naval quarantine around Cuban waters. In response to this move he received two mixed messages from the Soviets. The first was a tough hard-line message from the Kremlin and the second a far more conciliatory message apparently written by Premier Krushchev himself. In a wise negotiation tactic JFK ignored the first aggressive message from the Kremlin and responded only to the second more reasonable one. Following this direct dialogue, the ships turned back and the world breathed a sigh of relief.

JFK's brother, Robert Kennedy wrote a book about this episode called *Thirteen Days* [91]. In it he gives a close and personal account of the president's handling of the situation and an insight into how a leader at the higher end of personal cognitive development is able to

---

[91] Kennedy, R. (1971). *Thirteen Days: A Memoir of the Cuban Missile Crisis.* New York: W. W. Norton.

operate under such pressurised and ambiguous conditions.

For example, in leadership and diplomacy JFK knew the importance of being able to see and understand a situation from another's point of view. In the missile crisis this included both his adversaries and his advisors. He knew that he couldn't push the strong militarist forces in Moscow into a corner that left them no options to manoeuvre other than to go on the offensive. He also had to placate some of his own advisors, some of whom still thought they should attack even as the Soviet ships were retreating.

He also understood the need to cultivate allies. He knew that in the US versus the USSR his country was in a potentially weak and exposed position without strong international support. In cultivating this support, he was highly aware of the importance of both his own and US credibility and so was careful throughout the crisis to communicate honestly on all fronts. JFK was well-read and in this particular situation took sage advice he found in a

British military text called *Deterrent or Defence* [92],

"Keep strong, if possible, in any case keep cool. Have unlimited patience. Never corner an opponent and always assist him to save face. Put yourself in his shoes – so as to see things through his eyes" (p.277).

JFK thoughtfully cultivated a bipartisan group of advisors with broad and divergent views and sought their counsel during the crisis. It is generally believed that it was such personal and professional insight, maturity and wisdom that saved the world from a global catastrophe in 1962.

Leadership Development Levels

Constructive Developmental Theory [93] (CDT) is a theory of developing cognitive complexity. It relates to the maturity and sophistication of a person's meaning-making process and how they interpret and

---

[92] Hart, B. L. (2018). *Deterrent or Defence: A Fresh Look at the West's Military Position.* Pickle Partners Publishing. UK.

[93] Kegan, R. (1980). *Making Meaning: The Constructive-Developmental Approach to Persons and Practice.* The Personnel and Guidance Journal, 58, 373-380.

evaluate their experience. Such mental complexity directly influences the way in which an individual is able to perceive, understand and relate to the world around them. Under normal circumstances, a person's construction of meanings and interpretations grow more complex over time. The application of this theory to leadership is known as *Leadership Development Levels* [94].

Rather than focusing on the acquisition of discrete skills and knowledge, Leadership Development Levels (LDLs) describe a person's overarching complexity with which they understand themselves, their world and their leadership. They closely match the adult development levels but look at development specifically from the leadership perspective and are comprised of three domains, the: *Intrapersonal, Interpersonal* and *Cognitive*. Within the *Intrapersonal* domain the leader moves from an externally to an internally defined sense of self. In the *Interpersonal* domain they gradually move from a self to other focus. And in the *Cognitive* domain they move from

---

[94] Eigel, K. M., & Kuhnert, K. W. (2005). *Authentic Development: Leadership Development Level and Executive Effectiveness.* In Gardener, W., Avolio, B. and Walumba, F. (Eds) Authentic Leadership Theory and Practise: Origins, Effects and Development. Monographs in Leadership and Management, 3, Elsevier, Oxford, 357-385.

simplicity to complexity.

Movement through these levels is unidirectional, meaning that a leader cannot miss a stage, nor can they regress in their understanding. As such, each level encompasses the previous levels but then expands and extends to the next as earlier ways of meaning-making are integrated into more comprehensive and complex later ways. Although the direction of progress is universal, the speed and level of ultimate development will vary from one individual leader to another. It is helpful to think of it as the vertical-development of *how* we know versus the horizontal-development of *what* we know. Each level is defined as follows:

Leader Development Level 1 - Emphasis is on own needs, interests and wishes. These leaders are effective in straightforward environments using concrete and rule-driven strategies. This level represents the lowest or least sophisticated level of development. Leaders at this level view the world in very simplistic terms. They see it mainly as either black or white and miss the many subtle shades of grey in between. They struggle with paradox, ambiguity and even alternative viewpoints. These leaders have to operate by following strict and concrete rules that they in turn expect others to follow and so can prove quite ineffectual in modern VUCA environments (Volatile, Uncertain, Complex and Ambiguous). It is estimated less than 10% of today's leaders operate at this level.

Leader Development Level 2 - Emphasis on mutuality and interpersonal concordance. These leaders are effective in routine and stable environments using simple learned strategies. Leaders move to this level when they eventually learn the limitations of Level 1. They are now capable of recognising alternate viewpoints and the subtler shades of grey in situations. Although they are capable of accepting outside counsel, one drawback of this stage is that they may become reliant on it. They seek external opinion even on occasions when what is called for is their own internal guidance.

Leader Development Level 3 - Emphasis on personal autonomy, authorship and self-identity. These leaders are effective in novel environments and use integrated strategies in a self-authored way. At this level a leader's understanding starts to come more from within than without as they become more independent in thought and act. They continue to consider external information but now simply look upon it at it as one factor in the overall decision-making process. They develop a more complex understanding of the world and it is considered that transformational and authentic leadership begins at this level.

Leader Development Level 4 - Emphasis on individuality and inter-connectivity of systems. These leaders are effective in dynamic environments and use a deep-seated values orientation to evaluate multiple competing strategies. This is the highest level but one that only about 5% to 8% of leaders attain. A complete paradigm shift occurs here in that leaders start to welcome other paradigms. Here we could think of the likes of Bill Gates and what he achieved in the tech revolution with Microsoft, but then also what he has gone on to pioneer in philanthropic global healthcare through the Bill & Melinda Gates Foundation. These leaders ground themselves in their own vision and values but are completely capable of understanding and even integrating those of others. They have a capacity for the ambiguous, incomplete and paradoxical. And it is this complex and open view of themselves, others and the world that makes Level 4 leaders the most effective in the fast paced and dynamic VUCA conditions that characterise most modern environments. It is fair to assume JFK was a higher-level leader and was thus able to draw on this to successfully navigate both himself and his administration through the potentially cataclysmic Cuban missile crisis.

Although authentic behaviour can be witnessed at any level it is generally considered that transformative authentic leadership only really begins to occur at LDL 3&4 as it is here that leaders becoming truly self-authored. What level would you put your own individual development at? How are you with uncertainty, complexity and paradox? Can you tolerate the tension of contradictory ideas and polarities? What does this say about you and your leadership? Considering it is more life experience than classroom training that moves people through their vertical development, what do you think are the next important lessons for you to learn on your journey towards greater personal and leader authenticity?

Further Reading:

Fusco, T. et al (2016). *Authentic Leadership is not just about Ethical Leadership it's also about Strategic Leadership*. Coaching Psychology International. 9, 1. 4-10. The International Society of Coaching Psychology.

V is for **Values**

> *"Values have a transcendental quality, guiding actions, attitudes and judgements"* [95]

All leadership can be considered value-driven, inasmuch as an individual's leadership focus and style will inevitably be influenced by their own guiding personal and professional principles. The idea of leadership values has become particularly relevant with the increased focus on authentic leadership, but do we know what we mean when we talk about values? In this chapter we'll consider in detail some proposed definitions of values and value categories that have been identified through research in the field.

In a nutshell, values can be described as *abstract ideals* or *trans-situational principles* that guide our choices and

---

[95] Rokeach, M. (1973). *The Nature of Human Values.* Free Press. US.

behaviours and influence our evaluation of people and events. Values consciously and unconsciously mobilise and direct the decisions we make and are to a large extent derived, learned and internalised from society. Therefore, it is just as meaningful to talk of societal or ideological values as it is personal values. They emerge as human groups develop their particular preferences around obligatory behaviour and desirable conduct. In this way they meet the demands of both human nature and group functioning, as they promote cooperative and supportive relationships and develop commitment through group identification and loyalty. This makes it an important issue in authentic leadership, as values are not just psychological in nature, but also sociological and are present at an individual, team and organisational level.

Values then are learned and developed through the group experience of – approval/disapproval, gratification/deprivation, success/failure, etc. and are socially shared cognitive representations of desires, needs and goals. As such, in an ideal world, individual and group values would be different sides of the same coin. In *Understanding Human Values* [96]

---

[96] Schwartz, S. H. (2012). *An Overview of the Schwartz Theory of Basic Values.* Online readings in Psychology and Culture, *2* (1), 11.

Milton Rokeach explains,

> "Similar repeated and pervasive experiences are often characteristic of large numbers of persons… described, discussed and appraised by the persons involved… eventually building value standards, which often become widely accepted across social and cultural boundaries" (p.22).

As a result of this sharing, values become socially communicated conceptions of the desirable, the expected and the obligatory, and so they come to serve as standards. Standards that we learn to employ across situations that guide the views we hold with regards matters of community, education, religion, politics, ideologies etc. They are also standards that we use to evaluate and judge others as well as ourselves. It is also worth noting that values become inextricably linked to emotion. When our personal or group values are transgressed, we tend to respond not just rationally and cognitively, but also emotionally. Observe yourself when next a colleague says something that runs counter to a principle you hold dear. Perhaps it will be about trust, competence, transparency, fairness, respect, whatever it is, if there is a clear violation of a value you feel strongly enough about, you will very probably have a physiological response as well as an intellectual one.

Most of the significant research in this area has identified two overarching frameworks that most values seem to fall into. The first framework was developed by Schwartz [97] and allocates values into the two categories of *self-enhancement* and *self-transcendent* values. The second, developed by Rokeach[98] places them into *Terminal* and *Instrumental* value categories. Both are explored below.

The Schwartz framework identifies a total of ten values which, unlike morals and ethics, appear to be consistent cross-culturally:

Self-enhancement values emphasise the pursuit of one's own interests and are:

- Achievement – includes ambition/influence/success/skill/intelligence/competence.

---

[97] Rokeach, M. *(*2008*). Understanding Human Values.* Simon and Schuster. New York.

[98] Schwartz, S. H. (2012). *An Overview of the Schwartz Theory of Basic Values.* Online readings in Psychology and Culture, *2* (1), 11.

- Power – includes status/prestige/control/authority/social power/social recognition/public image.
- Stimulation – includes novelty/challenge/excitement/variety/daring.
- Self-direction – includes independence/exploring/creating/curiosity/autonomy/freedom/goals.
- Hedonism – includes personal pleasure/sensuous gratification/pleasure/enjoyment.

Self-transcendent values emphasise the welfare and interests of others and are:

- Universalism – includes understanding/appreciation/tolerance/welfare/equality/peace/wisdom/ beauty/nature/broad-mindedness/harmony/social justice.
- Benevolence – includes protection/loyalty/honesty/forgiveness/helpfulness/responsibility/ friendship.
- Tradition – includes respect/acceptance/commitment/tradition/moderation/humbleness/ acceptance.
- Conformity – includes restraint/obedience/politeness/self-discipline.

- Security – includes safety/harmony/stability/belonging/social-order/health/family-security.

It is interesting to note that a lot of writers and researchers almost instinctively place emphasis on the self-transcendent values for Authentic Leaders. Yet my own research (and that of others) clearly show that self-enhancement values, particularly achievement and self-direction, are both legitimate values in Authentic Leaders. It is also important, particularly in a discussion of authenticity, to emphasise that these are just value categories and they tell us nothing about the choice of category an individual should make, nor indeed the substantive content of the categories they do choose. For example, you may choose professional ambition or intellectual curiosity as a value, but it will be for you to decide what you are ambitious for or curious about. The group coaching approach to ALD is very powerful here, in that it doesn't tell you what values you should hold unlike many so-called Authentic Leadership 'training' programmes that seem to propose both value category and content, i.e.: self-transcendence > benevolence > honesty as one common example.

If real ALD seeks to genuinely develop authenticity, it has to leave the individual leader to be the main author of what it is they genuinely consider important in terms of their personal values. It's not beyond the realms of possibility that you'll end up discovering that you have a value that is held by or even suggested to you by another, but the point is that you have discovered it for yourself and, importantly, you will then have an understanding of why you hold this particular value. Take honesty, for example, within the Benevolence category again. Most people might agree that this is a useful and decent value to have and to encourage in the workplace and in teams. But honesty about what? As your manager, I may tell you I'm unconcerned if you help yourself to the contents of the stationery cupboard for your home office. However, I may be quite insistent about transparency in terms of your thoughts and feelings concerning work-based issues that are important to our team. One is fundamentally different from the other. So, it is important as a leader to understand the genesis of your values, so you can genuinely own them and act on them.

Next, the Rokeach value system comprises two categories of *terminal* and *instrumental* values.

Terminal values are composed of beliefs concerning ultimate goals and desirable end-states.

These include:

- A comfortable life (prosperous)
- An exciting life (stimulating and active)
- A sense of accomplishment (lasting contribution)
- A world at peace (free of war and conflict)
- A world of beauty (arts and nature)
- Equality (equal opportunities and brotherhood)
- Family security (taking care of loved ones)
- Freedom (independence and free choice)
- Happiness (contentedness)
- Inner harmony (freedom from inner conflict)
- Mature love (sexual and spiritual intimacy)
- National security (protection from attack)
- Pleasure (enjoyable and leisurely life)
- Salvation (a saved or eternal life)
- Self-respect (self-esteem)
- Social recognition (respect and admiration)
- Friendship (close companionship)
- Wisdom (mature understanding of life)

Instrumental values are concerned with modes of conduct or behaviour that are instrumental to the achievement of the desired terminal states above.

They include:

- Ambitious (aspiring and hard-working)
- Broadminded (open-minded)
- Capable (effective and competent)
- Cheerful (light-hearted and joyful)
- Clean (neat and tidy)
- Courageous (standing up for beliefs)
- Forgiving (pardoning others)
- Helpful (working for others welfare)
- Honest (sincere and truthful)
- Imaginative (daring and creative)
- Independent (self-reliant and self-sufficient)
- Intellectual (intelligent and reflective)
- Logical (rational and consistent)
- Loving (affectionate and tender)
- Obedient (dutiful and respectful)
- Polite (courteous and well-mannered)
- Responsible (reliable and dependable)
- Self-controlled (restrained and self-disciplined)

Whichever of the values above resonate with you, they will be highly significant in that they will both transcend and underpin your attitudes. But what happens when values come into conflict with each other?

"Actions in pursuit of a value… may conflict or may be congruent with the pursuit of other values. For example, the pursuit of achievement values may conflict with the pursuit of benevolence values – seeking success for self is likely to obstruct actions aimed at enhancing the welfare of others" [99] (p.2).

I had personal experience of this exact values conflict some years ago while working with an organisation in the UK. At that time the organisation was going through a restructuring to make it more commercial in its outlook and service. During one project I travelled the UK interviewing high street counter staff who were facing a change to their role that would see them on the front line trying to sell a variety of finance products to counter customers; home insurance, travel insurance etc. The requirement was that the counter staff would promote these new products quite aggressively with each and every customer interaction they had. In my interviews it became apparent that a vast majority of counter staff perceived their role as one of service to the public. This included values related to *Benevolence*, with its focus on the welfare of the customers and its

---

[99] Schwartz, S. H. (2007). *Basic Human Values: Theory, Methods and Applications*. Risorsa Uomo.

constituent values of; *honesty, helpfulness and responsibility*. However, in this new aggressive sales-orientated approach the counter staff were required to perform behaviour more based on the values of *achievement, power* and *goal success*. In addition, values of *tradition* were also transgressed on behalf of both the staff and customers. Needless to say, along with a considerable amount of unhappiness among their customer base, this situation created varying degrees of tension, resistance, confusion, apathy and even overt hostility among the frontline staff themselves.

As such, values can be a source of motivation, but value transgression or conflict can also be a source of demotivation, resistance and even hostility. Put simply, behaviours, actions and goals are more attractive to the degree that they promote the attainment of sought-after values. High priority values are central to an individual's self-concept. So, if you choose work goals for yourself and your team that are congruent with personal and group values then you tap into an intrinsic fount of natural motivation.

It may be a useful exercise to identify your top two or three values from each list above. Do you find them complimentary? Or are they in any way contradictory? Importantly, where from your own personal history do you think they come from? This is key as the roots of your personal and leadership authenticity lay deeply embedded in the values of your personal history and autobiography.

W is for Why?

There is an old tale of a business leader who allegedly said, "I know at least half of the money we spend on marketing is effective, I just don't know which half!" The situation I believe is the same for traditional training and development. Maybe there's simply too many variables between cause and effect that make it too complex to isolate the direct correlation between management & leadership development in the classroom and overall organisational performance.

The story is no different for Authentic Leadership development. In fact, it's probably worse. Due to the potentially ethereal perception of the term Authentic Leadership some people are understandably suspicious or cynical about the concept and its direct business or organisational benefits. I personally consider this perception fair, reasonable and inevitable and is therefore the precise reason I undertook my own research, to answer such concerns in as scientific a way as possible [100]. My research evaluating authentic leadership development was designed to provide empirical answers to three crucial questions about the group-coaching approach to ALD; does it work, how does it work and what does work actually mean? In short – *why* bother?

To fully understand the benefits of ALD I employed a Grounded Theory [101] method of evaluation to understand what the actual *output* of ALD group-coaching is and through this process I identified six authentic leadership *attributes*. These aren't skills or traits per se, they are more akin to qualities, but qualities that can, and do, lead to concrete behaviour change and performance improvement. What these 6 attributes represent are the common qualities that leaders develop having gone through the group-coaching program. Not everyone develops all of them, indeed not everyone needs to. But everyone who completes the program develops their own unique combination of the six which they in turn use in their own unique specific way, according to their

---

[100] Fusco, T. et al (2015). *Authentic Leaders are Conscious, Confident, Competent and Congruent.* A Grounded Theory of Authentic Leadership Group Coaching. International Coaching Psychology Review. 10, 2. 131-148. The British Psychological Society.

[101] Glaser, B. G. & Strauss, A. L. (1967). *The Discovery of Grounded Theory: Strategies for Qualitative Research.* New York: Aldine.

individual needs and priorities.

Employing the Grounded Theory method, data was coded and categorised from transcribed participant interviews three months after their groups had finished. The purpose of the timing was to leave a sufficient gap from their last ALD session to allow for the natural atrophy that invariably follows many leadership development interventions. The interviews were designed to gather data at three common levels of leadership development evaluation as discussed under 'O' (Organisation Development) - What did the leader learn? How has that changed their behaviour? How has that improved their performance? Astonishingly, longitudinal interviews conducted with many participants reveal that significant changes remain in place up to three years later. Systematic interrogation of the interview data identified six key outcomes from the group-coaching as follows:

1/ Self-understanding & Self-Regulation – This is a self-awareness that fosters greater self-control and mastery. It is an attribute that represents an increase in cognitive, emotional and motivational awareness. It also includes an increase in the effective self-regulation in each of these domains as a result of gaining greater insight into existing behaviour patterns and the development of potential and more effective alternatives. Interview extracts below give a sense of what insights this raised self-awareness and regulation promotes:

"I do stop myself and give myself more time to think now. Normally my attitude has been quite cavalier about things, if it feels right then let's do it. But since the programme, I've actually been giving myself time to reflect and think more deeply about things. This now often leads to completely different views of things and has positively impacted some pretty major decisions."

2/ Interpersonal Understanding – This attribute is a greater understanding of a leader's interpersonal domain and includes an appreciation and understanding of the different styles and behaviours of others. This may include colleagues and clients but is particularly pertinent to the people they lead.

"I'm much better with challenge now. I would never say I was poor with people and didn't have time for people, but I wasn't as good as I could be. Sometimes I didn't exhibit the right behaviour towards them. I just think I'm much better at that now and so even quite difficult conversations don't feel like things that are going to get pushed back to a different time and are now things that we can have in a very mature fashion"

3/ Relationship Management – This is an ability to adapt to the styles and behaviours of others. This attribute is built on the previous one, where an individual takes a new understanding of their interpersonal domain and uses this to inform new and more effective ways of communicating and relating to others.

"It's really helped me knowing the team and one guy in particular who just seems to fly off all over the place. He's doing a million things and I really struggle to understand what he's asking me sometimes. But recognising and understanding him now helps me work better with him. I could have just got completely frustrated with him and probably stopped dealing with him. Whereas now I'm prepared to take time out to understand what it is he needs from me to help him."

4/ Purposeful Leadership – This is the deliberate and proactive approach to an individual's leadership role. This attribute also includes an increase in an individual's focus and resilience in how they approach and execute their leadership responsibilities. Without actually teaching new management skills it appears the group process and self-reflection removes intrinsic blockers that in turn enable an individual to engage more fully and effectively with their work.

"I can't pick out a point at which I said to myself - yes I'm going to do something about my self-confidence, but something's happened throughout the program where I've gone, 'yeah, I'm going to have a go at that' and without even thinking about it I've volunteered for various things. That's thrown me into some challenges, but they've all been met OK. An option going forward is that I get the entire site reporting into me rather than through each of the Directorates. If you'd offered me that a few months ago – I'd have thought, oh my god - I don't want 100 extra people working for me! But yeah, I want that now."

5/ Conscious Leadership – This attribute relates to a more confident and considered approach to the role of leadership itself and becomes apparent when individuals begin to look less at the technical management aspects of their role and more assuredly at the point and purpose of their own personal leadership.

"I'm much clearer on what I'm doing now and much clearer on what I need to do to be successful in the leadership role I'm doing. Both in terms of the team I lead and also in terms of support for my own leadership team. I'm much clearer about my expectations from staff and they now know exactly where they are with me now and if I don't like something I see, I tell them very directly. I can deliver those messages now with greater clarity which means they're also stepping up now too, which is great."

6/ Strategic Leadership – This represents a broad and long-term leadership focus and is clear evidence that this approach to ALD helps leaders move up through the Leadership Development Levels that we looked at under 'U' (Uncertainty). It shows an increased capacity to turn the two previous categories into strategic action, taking the increase in leadership confidence and clarity and translating it into important long-term goals. The group coaching offers no actual training in strategic thinking or strategic planning but, as with the other attributes, this emerges quite clearly and consistently.

"I've created more time to do the corporate stuff that I avoided a bit before, so I spend more time looking-up rather than just organising-down. It's more considered and strategic. For example, when I started to form this new team I said - let's get the strategy right in terms of what we are here to do. Let's put in place the right machinery, behaviours and culture to drive that strategy and get the program of activities right so we know what steps we need to take to deliver that strategy."

The final step in fully coding and categorising the ALD output data into demonstrable leadership qualities made it apparent that they each relate to one another in various ways. For example, an increased understanding of others can also lead to more effective interactions with them. An increase in conscious and purposeful leadership can increase a focus on strategic leadership, and so on. On this basis an over-arching four-component model of Authentic Leadership was developed (Fig.1).

Fig.1: Four Component Model of Authentic Leadership

CONSCIOUS Leadership	**COMPETENT** Leadership
CONFIDENT Leadership	**CONGRUENT** Leadership

This research then resulted in a four-component model of Authentic Leader that describes an authentic leader as one that is: a *Conscious leader* that is deliberate and intentional, a *Competent leader* that is skilled and able; a *Confident leader* that is assertive and self-assured; and a *Congruent leader* that is clear and consistent. This research data has been further advanced and developed into the ALD:360® which is a self-assessment and 360-degree instrument that participants can use to track the focus and extent of their development through their ALD experience [102].

---

[102] Fusco, T. (2018). *Authentic Leadership Development: Some Philosophical, Theoretical and Practical Dilemmas answered through Group-Coaching and the ALD360®* . Philosophy of Coaching: An International Journal. 3, 2. 60-79.

X is for **Xenophile**

As you can imagine dear reader, X was a bit of a challenge and so this is a bit of a leap! Xenophilia, however, is defined as an attraction to foreign cultures, customs and people. So, the leap I make is to illustrate how meaningful Authentic Leadership Development can help individual leaders understand, appreciate and even embrace the seemingly foreign culture and customs of the 'others' they have to engage, lead and work alongside.

The fundamental premise of the ALD coaching group is very different from the leadership classroom or lecture theatre. It is not about learning from management models, leadership theory or business case studies. By the time a leader is ready to enter an ALD coaching group they may well have done all of these extensively. The coaching-group therefore is about experiencing and understanding yourself and others more deeply. It is about reflecting on what leadership means to you personally and gaining a sense of the personal identity that guides that leadership. It can come as nothing short of a culture shock when you explore all of this with others in the ALD group. It both invites and forces you to thoughtfully consider *the other*; the other style, the other view, the other ambition, the other values, the other practice, the other experience. And what does this achieve? Well of course it naturally makes you consider, and sometimes reconsider, your own; style, views, values, ambition, practice and experience, in comparison and contrast to those others. It can take you from a place of confusion and frustration about *others* to a place where you understand and even appreciate and embrace what these *others* have to offer. Listen to some participant observations below that offer a sense of how this learning unfolds throughout the group process:

I now recognise that a breadth of humanity can be effective in successfully delivering outcomes. I knew this hypothetically but to be confronted with it by people in the group was another thing altogether. I think I've learnt how to listen to people with less judgement, it's dawned on me that there is a place for all of these different styles, and one is not necessarily better than the other. I guess in the past I made the assumption that everyone functions in pretty similar ways, but I realise now that people absolutely don't. It was great to listen to the others, particularly those that function in very different ways to me and hear about how that effectively serves them. The diversity in the group was amazing in terms of how differently we all operate and to have that opportunity to share quite deeply about our own experiences of how we operate was incredibly valuable. When we had the time to explain why we are the way we are, and why we feel the way we feel about certain things and life experiences and the paths we've taken fundamentally changed the way I think about others. Just thinking my way was the right way was just arrogance. I have a much greater respect now for other people generally than perhaps I did previously. I knew that I should value people's differences, but I find I'm actually more willing and able to do that now. I've fundamentally learnt that people really are different. Even though I supposedly knew this and knew that I was supposed to know this! Other people you work with tell you it and I even tell other people it. But now for the first time I really understand it and believe it genuinely.

And how this learning can manifest back in the workplace…

I can now identify much better how other people around me are operating. Everyone has their own way of doing things and I'm far clearer on where the strengths of other people around me lay, which is fascinating. Some within my team have similar character types to myself and I'd usually gravitate towards them when I wanted the job done. We'd work out the plan and then we'd tell the others what to do. I've realised now that different people have different ways of thinking about things. And it's about trying to learn the value of their input. This point about people having different styles and using that, I think I did before to a degree but I've become much more aware of the fact that you really do need to do that, and that you need to flex your own style too. So that's something I've started to do now, and I'll continue to as I can already feel it coming more and more naturally to me. Something else is that I can understand people better and understand why they decide things the way they do. I may not always agree with it, but I make more effort to understand why they're doing it their particular way. To recognise - 'yes you are different to me and we have different ways of doing things, but I understand why you're approaching it like that'. This is dramatically improving both our interactions and outcomes.

These sorts of interpersonal insights and shifts can only take place when working intensely in the company of others, for it is they that are the catalysts of your learning. The effectiveness of the group-coaching approach to ALD is due in large part to the opportunity it affords participants to work on the development of their authentic *self* within a social context. According to the theories of Social Psychology the self is gradually formed in interaction with the world. We build a sense of self through our interactions with our significant others and groups. An individual self is developed and nurtured in ongoing *contrast and comparison* to others in the world around us. However, other theories of the *self* suggest it actually has a dual aspect that operates at two levels simultaneously. There is also the internally organised element that deals with self-relevant issues such as our thoughts, emotions, motivations etc. It is suggested this develops independently of the socially constructed self. The group-coaching process is able to meet both of these aspects developing both this intra-personal self along with the inter-personal self [103] concurrently as individuals operate in both of these domains interchangeably within the group.

This group-coaching format represents the first scientifically evidenced approach to authentic leadership development available.

More information can be found at www.authenticleadershipdevelopment.co.uk.

---

[103] Fusco, T. et al (2016). *Increasing Leaders Self-Concept-Clarity in the Authentic Leadership Coaching Group*. The Coaching Psychologist. 12, 2. 24-32. The British Psychological Society.

Y is for **Yalom**

If you the reader have had your interest piqued by any of the ideas presented throughout this book, particularly those relating to existentialism, I can make no better recommendation than to investigate the works of the American psychotherapist Irvin Yalom. Yalom pioneered something that he calls the *teaching novel*. These are books that offer an almost effortless introduction to the world of existential and group psychotherapy. Among them are the intriguing titles of; The Schopenhauer Cure and The Spinoza Problem. He blends insights from such philosophers as these with his own individual approach to therapy. As such, his philosophic therapy is not based on a pathological or medical therapy [104] (despite him being an MD and Psychiatrist). His approach is to explore his clients own personal experience of their natural, if sometimes troubling, human condition. He believes his clients are not ill, but are lost, confused or stalled. He doesn't consider their concerns as medical maladies but more natural philosophical concerns or anxieties arising from how they are perceiving and orientating themselves to their worlds (I personally found that this made a perfect model on which to build a meaningful approach to authentic leadership development). In addition, he also gives the reader an extremely intimate glimpse into his working relationship with his clients and what is unfolding for them both during their encounters. This he does exquisitely through his novels which though based on actual client encounters, unfold with all the drama and intrigue worthy of any fiction.

However, despite all this, it's not Yalom's excellent teaching novels that concern us here. Rather, it is his pioneering work and research as a group therapist. For it was in this capacity, working particularly at the John Hopkins Hospital, that he identified some of the critical conditions that made his group work so

---

[104] Yalom, I. (1980). *Existential Psychotherapy*. New York: Basic Books.

effective. This also gives us insight into how and why the group-coaching approach to ALD works as effectively as it does [105]. Two of these factors are *psychological safety* and *group cohesion*.

Group Cohesion is desirable to any important group endeavour but is critical for effective group-therapy, group-coaching and group ALD. If you want people to explore their personal and professional values, ambitions, goals and anxieties along with their own self-concept and leadership identity, they must experience psychological safety and group cohesion. For those of you that have experienced one-to-one coaching you will know that the coaching relationship you experience is a key factor to coaching success. As it happens, just prior to writing this chapter I conducted a 'chemistry session' with a potential new coachee over the telephone. By the end of the call he said he was keen to progress saying that he felt comfortable with my attitude, style and approach. It seems therefore within the duration of that call I was able to create the necessary conditions under which this new coachee will be willing and able to engage in the uncompromising self-reflection and exploration that coaching requires. This is just as important for

---

[105] Yalom, I., Leszcz, M. (2005). *The Theory and Practice of Group Psychotherapy*. Basic Books: NY.

group work but is inevitably more complex.

First, psychological safety is achieved by the introduction of the Rogerian qualities discussed under 'R' that include; trust, empathic understanding, acceptance and unconditional positive regard. The introduction and unfaltering adherence to these qualities are what creates the psychological safety. When this experience of safety is shared by the group members individually and collectively, this is what creates group cohesion. Group cohesion can be thought of as the group equivalent of the effective working alliance that needs to be established in the one-to-one coaching relationship, but more complex due to the numbers and levels of variables involved. What this means is that there needs to be cohesiveness between the group members and the group coach; between each of the individual group members themselves, and finally between the individual and the group as a whole. When this web of safety and cohesion is achieved, and each group member in turn feels accepted, valued and supported by the rest of the group (and this whole process is held and contained by the group coach) then they will feel able to engage in the important and self-reinforcing exploratory process of: self-disclosure – empathy – acceptance – trust – self-disclosure. This will then allow each group participant to engage in the past/present/future exploration that ALD involves to help individual leaders explore their personal values, strengths, weaknesses, ambitions and goals based on an honest and frank assessment of the history that formed them, the present they live and operate in, and the future to which they aspire.

Further Reading:

Yalom, I. D. (2014). *Lying on the Couch*. Basic Books. US.

Yalom, I. D. (2012). *The Spinoza Problem*. Hachette. UK.

Yalom, I. D. (2005). *The Schopenhauer Cure*. Scribe Publications. US.

Yalom, I. D. (1989). *Love's Executioner, and Other Tales of Psychotherapy*. New York: Harper Perennial.

Z is for Zeitgeist

"Boundary experiences instigate a radical shift in life perspective" [106]

I write this final chapter amidst the Coronavirus pandemic. As it stands it looks like all the clichés will prove accurate. It IS a once in a generation experience, and it WILL lead to a new normal. And as nearly half a million die, the riots blaze across America and Hong Kong, the US and China descend into a new Cold War and great depression levels of unemployment become common, the world stares out towards a very, very uncertain future. Our current zeitgeist, the spirit of our times, really does feel like the world has shifted on its axis. But we will survive, adjust and ultimately prosper once again – we always have.

A rather innocuous and frankly pointless TV

---

[106] Yalom, I. (1980). *Existential Psychotherapy*. New York: Basic Books.

advertisement around this time, for a product I no longer recall, contained a profound yet deceptively simple message within it - "As we all think about rushing back to normal, it is worth considering what of the old normal is worth rushing back to". As an existentialist by nature, it was within hours of the British Prime Minister announcing our lockdown that I began to ponder this question. Yet, to my astonishment, I saw a news article at about the 2-month mark of lockdown saying that during this period between 3% to 5% of Americans had had a life epiphany during this period. What?! What had the other 315 million people been thinking about during lockdown!? As discussed in the opening letters of the alphabet, modern life conspires to preoccupy us and keep us distracted away from such deep thinking. Advertisers and social media simply don't like it! But when you are effectively under house arrest what else *do* you think about? Sure, we're all faced with survival-related anxieties; finance, jobs, health – but these concerns contribute to such an existential shock therapy that they should help not hinder a fundamental revision of what we're doing in our lives and careers. It represents nothing short of what philosophers Karl Jaspers and Irvin Yalom call a boundary experience. A boundary experience is "… *an urgent experience that propels one into a confrontation with one's existential situation in the world*" [107] (p.159). It is an experience that forces you to confront your own personal existence and to seriously consider, as in the current zeitgeist – what are the fundamental priorities of my life – what from my old life do I want to rush back to?! To conclude this book, we are going to consider Irvin Yalom's main *ultimate concern* to see how this might guide us through our profound boundary experience and towards a wise, meaningful and authentic return to normal. This *ultimate concern* of Yalom's is the deceptively life-affirming contemplation of the ultimate boundary experience - *Death!*

Experiencing this global pandemic is to experience many forms of death. There are the many human actual deaths and near-deaths, experienced by hundreds of thousands, shared and witnessed by countless more. Then there is the end and interruption of other things, smaller voluminous deaths. Jobs, careers, ways of working, whys of working, hobbies, holidays, ways of being in our communities and ways of being with our friends and families. Other than in times of war I don't think so many people worldwide have confronted head-on

---

[107] Yalom, I. (1980). *Existential Psychotherapy*. New York: Basic Books.

their own personal boundary situation, so collectively.

The Stoic philosophers of ancient Greece believed that death was the most important event in life and without it, life would lose much of its intensity – it shrinks. In *Existential Psychotherapy* [108] Yalom makes the point that although the biological life-death boundary is relatively precise, psychologically speaking, life and death merge into one another – death is inextricably a part of life. The central idea of this 500-page book, for me, comes down to one puncturing insight – *although the physicality of death destroys man, the idea of death saves him!* Yalom believes that death is of such monumental importance that if properly confronted, it can "… *alter one's life perspective and promote a truly authentic immersion in life*" (p.187). Boundary experiences of exposure to real death or metaphorical death can *wake* us. Wake us from our sleep-walk through life to a more authentic and conscious way of being. When you become more aware of mortality you often become primed to make significant changes to embrace life more fully, "*You are prompted to grapple with your fundamental human responsibility to construct an authentic life of engagement, connectivity, meaning,*

---

[108] Yalom, I. (1980). *Existential Psychotherapy*. New York: Basic Books.

and self-fulfilment" [109] (p.34). And boundary experiences are often exactly what it takes to achieve this transformation. For the various reasons described throughout this book it can take a herculean effort to become more aware and mindful, "*There are certain unalterable, irremediable conditions, certain 'urgent experiences' that jolt one, that tug one from the everyday state of existence to the state of mindfulness of being*" [110] (p.31). And this spirit of our time is certainly such an 'urgent experience' that offers us the chance (amid the emergency) to breathe an existential breath and take stock.

Many readers may understandably think that to conclude the alphabet on the subject of endings and death is a somewhat dismal and disheartening message. If that's the case, then a lot of the preceding messages have failed their function. Consider Frankl's key message (and the Stoics before him) that it is not things and events themselves that disturb us, but rather what we think about those things and events. The very real losses of this time are not to be denied or diminished, but what remains is perhaps to be revaluated. Even our smaller personal experiences of

---

[109] Yalom, I. D. (2008). *Staring at the Sun: Overcoming the Terror of Death*. San Francisco: Jossey-Bass.

[110] Yalom, I. (1980). *Existential Psychotherapy*. New York: Basic Books.

interruption can be profoundly difficult. But such collapse and confusion leave us ultimately with little choice. To turn this quietus into mere repose. That is, turn what might seem like a finishing stroke into a calm composure, in which to earnestly contemplate what of our normal is worthy of revisit. In this respect, the prospect of ending this book reflecting on such an ultimate concern is not meant as a message of dismay but of opportunity and optimism - to reassess and renew a meaningful acquaintance with life.

As I heard on a webinar this very afternoon with an ex-futurologist from British Telecom - *"You should never waste a crisis!"*.

Be well!

Further Reading:

Wallraff, C. F. (1970). *Karl Jaspers: An Introduction to his Philosophy*. Princeton University Press, New Jersey.

ABOUT THE AUTHOR

Dr Tony Fusco is a Chartered Psychologist specialising in leadership coaching and Authentic Leadership Development. His dissatisfaction with his professions attempts to earnestly tackle genuine authentic leadership development led him to develop the fields first scientific approach to Authentic Leadership Development. Research findings supporting the effectiveness of this group-coaching approach to ALD have been published in various British Psychological Society Journals and a 2018 Routledge book *'An Evidenced-Based Approach to Authentic Leadership Development'*.

Printed in Great Britain
by Amazon